Don Mullan, Director of AFrI, on *Famine Diary*

Gerald Keegan describes vividly the appalling conditions endured by Irish refugees aboard the infamous coffin ships. He helps us understand that every statistic was, in fact, a thinking, feeling and precious human being.

A comprehension of their suffering is, I believe, essential to the recovery of the soul of the Irish worldwide. They teach us that we cannot be indifferent to the suffering of the poor of Asia, Africa and Latin America. Indeed, the cry of the poor today, coming from the so-called 'Third World', is clearly telling us that the Rich World, to which the Irish now belong, is inflicting on their people the same political and economic injustices which our own people endured under British Colonialism at the time of the Great Irish 'Famine'.

Famine Diary is a book which every Irish person should read, including those who make decisions about our Official Development Assistance to the so-called 'Third World'.

Don Mullan, Director
Action From Ireland

Marianna O'Gallagher, Canadian publisher, on *Famine Diary*

There is a gentleness about this book that belies the horror of the underlying facts. Gerald Keegan's diary, which is the soul of the book, is a distillation of the centuries that preceded Yeats' "A Terrible Beauty". The young man who was sensitive to the beauty of language and poetry, evident in his phrasing; sensitive to humanity, evident in his love for his students and in his expressions of grief after his young wife died; sensitive to the cause of justice in his last wish that his diary go out to the world; this young man is the other side of the coin of Irish pain. We have become too familiar, almost bored, with violence in Ireland to the point where we cannot see "the other side of the coin" — look backwards into the history that made a people, look around us at the humane efforts that are being exercised by Irish men and women and their descendants around the globe in the cause of justice.

Brother James Mangan FSC deserves our thanks for carrying out Keegan's desire. May this accomplishment by an admiring fellow teacher bring eternal rest to Keegan and his generation; may it be example and encouragement to those who speak and work for justice.

Marianna O'Gallagher
Quebec

FAMINE
DIARY

FAMINE
DIARY

Journey to a New World

Gerald Keegan

Edited and presented by
James J. Mangan, FSC

Wolfhound Press

Reprinted 1991
This edition first published 1991 by
Wolfhound Press
68 Mountjoy Square
Dublin 1

The first printed version of Keegan's diary was published in 1895, in Quebec, under the title *Summer of Sorrow*. James Mangan's edited version was first published as *The Voyage of the Naparima* in 1982, by Carraig Books, Quebec.

Wolfhound Press receives financial assistance from The Arts Council/An Chomhairle Ealaíon, Dublin, Ireland.

British Library Cataloguing in Publication Data
Keegan, Gerald
   Famine diary: journey to a new world.
   1. Ireland. Emigrants. Canada
   I. Title II. Mangan, James J.
   304.8710415

ISBN 0-86327-300-9

Cover design by Jan de Fouw
Typesetting by Phototype-Set Ltd.
Printed by the Guernsey Press Co. Ltd.,
Guernsey, Channel Islands.

Contents

Introduction

About ten years ago I received authorization from the Canadian Department of Agriculture to visit Grosse Ile. The scene of a mass tragedy in 1847, the island has been closed to the public for about seventy-five years.

The object of my visit was to see the historic site at the west end of the island. The burial trenches where thousands of Irish emigrants were laid to rest and the monuments, one next to the graveyard and the other on "Telegraph Hill", occupy this corner of Grosse Ile.

It was a never-to-be-forgotten sight to look across the rows of burial trenches, their outline marked by a hollowing of the surface above each row. In memory I went back to the summer of 1847 when cart-loads of bodies were dumped pell-mell, one of top of the other, in an endless procession from the fever sheds. This was the final indignity, the last of a whole series of bitter disappointments and bitter sufferings, that these emigrants were subjected to in their flight from famine, fever and persecution at home.

The facts about the mistreatment of the emigrants both

during their voyage across the ocean and upon their landing in Canada were so shocking that the government of the day tried in every way possible to keep the public from finding out what was going on.

Gerald Keegan was one of these emigrants who made the long voyage across the Atlantic, and saw the shocking conditions on Grosse Ile. The diary he kept was first published in Huntingdon, Quebec, in 1895, but was apparently censored by the government. It was simply too frank an exposure of the injustices that were at the root of the emigration movement. Somehow the ban was effective. There is no known copy of the publication in Canada today, as far as can be found as a result of a rather detailed search. My photostat copy became the inspiration and the main theme of the story that follows.

In editing and presenting Keegan's diary, I wished to make it intelligible to readers who might not be familiar with the historical background of the mass emigration movement from Ireland in 1847. Therefore, substantial additions were made while every precaution was taken to maintain the charming simplicity and frankness of the author. The language idiom was changed to a more modern type of expression. The intensity of emotional overtones was somewhat reduced since it tended to distract the reader from the core of the message the author tried to convey. While the journal contains priceless eyewitness details on the fate of the emigrants as they were moved from Ireland to Canada, it had to be expanded so as to give a more complete picture of the meaning of the Grosse Ile tragedy. Used in this way it became an excellent medium for presenting the picture.

Due to the revision and additions, dates had to be changed. As a result there may be a few inconsistencies in the time allowed for some of the events in the story to take place. For example there may not have been enough time allowed for the emigrants to march from Sligo to

Dublin. By taking into account the fact that the boats were always a week or so late in departing, this discrepancy may be permissible. In other words, some may have taken several extra days and still have been on time.

In order to fill out the historical background of the emigration movement a number of characters were introduced in *Famine Diary*. In fact the only names in the beginning of the journal that are not fictitious are the names of the author, Keegan, and the first name of his bride, Eileen. On Grosse Ile, however, the names of the doctors and clergy are their real names. There are a few possible exceptions. The names of two or three of the clergy are doubtful since different records give different lists.

This diary shows us the human face of the statistics of the famine dead. We know about the cruelty of the landlords, but life aboard the coffin ships is hardly documented and the ultimate fate of the emigrants is rarely adverted to.

However, what is most heart-rending and awe-inspiring about Keegan's story is the spirit and humanity of a starving people – they gave what little they had to others and never accepted their fate as the will of God, knowing that their misery was a direct result of the evil machinations of their overlords, who allowed an entire nation to starve in a land of plenty.

The reader need not expect that *Famine Diary* will be a nice story. In fact it is a kind of horror story. Some people might be inclined to suggest that we should forget all about the dark pages of history, about events like the Grosse Ile tragedy and how it came about, and let them remain buried in the past. I feel, however, that we need these stories both as reminders of the presence of good and evil in the world and for their human interest value in depicting helpless masses of the poor and the dispossessed fighting against what appear to be insurmountable odds.

James J. Mangan FSC

1

Black '47

*I've heard whisper of a country
That lies beyond the sea,
Where rich and poor stand equal
In the light of freedom's day.*

(Anon.)

Gerald Keegan made the first entry in his journal on February 18, 1847.

February 18. I am beginning this journal today in the hope that it will be a message to the world from this downtrodden land of ours. I realize that it may never get beyond the confines of this little village in County Sligo. In that case I will at least have the satisfaction of putting my thoughts into words. They are the words of a poor village schoolmaster, one of the two thousand tenants on Lord Palmerston's huge estate.

If the outside world only knew the facts about Ireland's condition I know that we would get help. The news that is getting out, mainly from the London *Times*, is a complete distortion of what is actually going on. I am determined to write down everything that strikes me as the reality of our situation.

The weather on this bleak, cold February day is in tune with the mood and the state of the people all over the land. What is most heartrending to me is the sad plight of the children.

Today when I told my cousin, Timmy O'Connor, to put out his hand for punishment for neglecting to do any work all week he said: "It's not that I meant it, sir. It's the belly gripe that I feel all the time and I can't do any work." The tears in his eyes overwhelmed me. I am shocked at myself for even thinking of any kind of punishment for neglect of duty. What is duty after all when people are literally tortured by the pangs of hunger? When school was out I slipped a penny into Timmy's hand to buy a scone at the baker's. If I only had enough from my salary to feed the hollow-cheeked, listless creatures in my school I'd feel it worthwhile to continue trying to teach them. Not a single one of them today was free from the ravages of hunger. Six have already died this winter so far and the rest are just hanging on. Several who should be here cannot come because they have no clothing to wear.

I can't help but wonder if there is any tribe of human beings in any part of the world reduced to the level of the people in Ireland today. It can hardly be possible. We have come to the end of our rope. The twin spectres, famine and pestilence, hold sway over the land. To judge by the news that is reaching us, people are dying so fast that their surviving relatives are unable to bury them all. Every thatched cottage and every rude shelter is in mourning. Pestilence would not be claiming so many lives if it were not for the famine. It is such a contradiction that, in one of the richest agricultural lands in the world, people are dying of hunger. They are not allowed to consume the products of the soil except for potatoes and sometimes turnips and cabbage. Thousands of tons of the best of food are being shipped, under armed guard, from every port in Ireland. We are the victims of England's economic policies.

February 19. When I came to my boarding house after school today Mrs Moriarty, my landlady, told me that my Uncle Jeremiah was coming over to see me. Poor man, he must be coming to ask for some help to keep Timmy and the two girls alive. But I won't have a shilling in my pocket till the board pays my quarterly salary, if indeed my allowance could be called a salary.

The drawn and haggard look of Jeremiah when he came to the door left me in no doubt about his own half-starved condition. Many of the parents in this area are starving themselves in an attempt to keep their children alive. I got Mrs Moriarty to roast another herring and serve it to him with a cup of tea. It was pitiful to watch him trying to show restraint while eating even though his hands were trembling from his eagerness to swallow the bit of food.

It turned out that he did not come to borrow or beg but to talk of emigration. He claimed that the whole country was in the throes of a mass emigration movement to Canada. I knew about it myself but I also know that it is, deep down, a forced expulsion under a plan conceived and now being executed by the landlords. But Jeremiah, like thousands of others, was tricked by the landlords' offer of paid passage to Canada and a grant of land together with a cash payment upon arrival. Knowing these people as I do, I am convinced that their offer is merely bait to get the poor tenants off the land and I am sure that the terms of the offer will be ignored by them. Nevertheless Uncle Jeremiah's enthusiasm is understandable. He has a family to feed and if some kind of help doesn't come soon they will all be dead.

February 20. I walked a considerable distance last night after Uncle Jeremiah left to try to get my thoughts into focus. Even though it looks like a solution, I am opposed to emigration. First of all it is being promoted by a ruthless, greedy group of landlords who wish to rid their vast estates of the helpless, starving, disease-ridden tenants whose desperate condition is a direct result of the seizure of their land and its produce by a foreign power. I spoke to several men in the village and, to judge by what they say, the landlords are succeeding in their concerted scheme. The people have taken the bait. Things are so far advanced that some boats are scheduled to sail in a few weeks. *Alea jacta est!* The die is cast. This is nothing short of a panic situation. Those who are behind the movement have chosen the right moment. Starving from an artificially created famine and disease-ridden as a result of hunger, the poor people are easy victims. The ravages of fever and dysentery are particularly acute at this time. Most of the people are in no condition to travel. A lot will surely die on the way to whatever destination they are heading for.

It is, indeed, beyond my powers of understanding that there should be any mention of emigration from the fertile green valleys of Ireland which is, agriculturally, one of the most productive countries in the world.

February 21. It is true that there is a potato famine in practically every part of the country but there is corn and wheat and meat and dairy products in abundance. For putting his hands on any of this, the tenant is liable to prison, even to execution or to exile.

Ireland has had several famines already in this century. Though they took a heavy toll in suffering and death they were far less severe than this one which is now in its second year. It is much more destructive than any preceding one. The destroying fungus that caused the failure of our potato crop was known in Europe long before it reached us. For the Europeans it amounted merely to a serious inconvenience. In our country where all the rest of our produce is seized and shipped mainly to England, the loss of the potato crop is a disaster. It is the sole item of diet for close to half the population.

The destroying fungus first appeared as a white fuzz on the under side of the potato leaves. The fungus quickly spread to the stem and to the potato itself. At the beginning nobody was alarmed for most of the crop a year ago last fall was considered good enough to harvest. It was stored in the customary pits and roothouses. Only those who delayed too long lost their crop but they knew that they could rely on help from any of the neighbours who had a good crop. It looked as if we could survive the winter all right.

But the pits were examined regularly as there was general uneasiness. When it was finally discovered that the blight was rotting the whole crop, all of us became alarmed. Uncle Jeremiah's pit contained about fifty barrels of what appeared to be a dependable winter's supply of food for his family. By the end of November it had all turned to a mass of rotten pulp. He was able to pick out less than one barrel of edible potatoes. It seems that no part of the country was spared. The winter of 1845 brought us the first wave of famine and its twin destroyer, pestilence. Those who lived near the fishing areas survived in greater numbers than the ones who lived far inland. When spring came the survivors lived on the promise of another growing season. But in many parts of the country there were no seed potatoes despite the widespread sharing on the part of those who had some.

It was painful during the time of severe hunger and disease to observe the effects of these twin spectres on the people. Despite what I consider the inimitable, almost unquenchable, inner strength with which my fellow-countrymen face the contingencies of life, the severity of the famine is taking its toll on their endurance. They are becoming listless and indifferent. And, strange to say, it is this hunger-stricken, discouraged, oppressed citizen of our fair land who is being accused, chiefly by the London *Times,* of being lazy, truculent and aimless. And this tune is being picked up by the world at large, it seems. Deprived of all the basic rights of free human beings and, above all, of the ownership and produce of the land on which he has to live as a tenant, he is supposed, by some strange wizardry, to be energetic and self-supporting and resigned to his lot.

The potato crop in the fall of 1846 was another failure. Those who planted a crop in the hope that the blight was over reaped only disappointment. The destroying fungus glutted itself on the pits leaving the people to face the winter on whatever fish they could get, together with some crop remnants of turnips and cabbage. I am speaking now of the two thousand tenants of Lord Palmerston's estate here in Sligo but reliable reports tell us that no part of the country has been spared. The scourge of famine has struck the west and the south with greater fury than elsewhere.

February 22. I feel more and more disheartened each day as I enter my little school. Some day soon I will have to tell the children to stay at home. Somehow I feel they are perplexed and mystified about what is going on, about what they and their parents and friends are enduring. But I would merely be adding to their anguish if I were to explain that we are under the crushing force of a relentless, immoral political machine, and that greedy landlords, most of them foreigners, are occupying and controlling all of the fertile land of our country. Historically, I could remind them that the artificially generated famine that we are now enduring is just one more among many disasters that have weighed upon us during the past four centuries during which time we have been reduced from a state of relative prosperity to one of destitution. I can ask them, however, to see the lie in what our enemies would have us believe and that is the blasphemous idea that all our troubles are a direct visitation of Divine Providence rather than the product of man's malice. Of late I have been conscious of my duty to try to keep their spirits alive in their frail, wasted bodies. But even that seems impossible now as their numbers become smaller each month.

February 23. Together with Tim Maloney, an ardent patriot, and a few other friends, I have some regular sources of information. Between them and a few newspapers we come across, we are getting a picture of the reality of these dark days.

The most disheartening effect of the intense sufferings of the people is a kind of despair and a sense of hopelessness that they are beginning to show. The average Irishman is a lover of conversation, music, poetry and even of leprechauns, so symbolic of the spirit world in which we like to roam. But all of these, together with the saving gift of seeing the humorous side to even the most desperate situation, is giving way to an alarming indifference to what fate has seemingly decreed for us. When severely deprived of the necessities of life, human beings have been known to lose all sense of decency to the extent of becoming predators, killing and robbing others so that they might survive. Though my people have been brought to as low a level of existence as is possible I feel thankful for the fact that they have preserved their sense of decency. It is true that there are cases of beastly behaviour but they are very rare. An English lady who recently travelled through some of the wild mountainous areas of the northwest, where she came across some of the desperately poor and hungry, claimed that she felt safer among them than on the streets of London.

Tim Maloney's answer to the mess that we are in is that we must take some kind of counter action against the forces that are destroying us. He favours the Young Ireland Movement, a successor to the many secret societies that have raised a hand against the forces of oppression in the past. Convinced that we will have to put up with just as much as we ourselves will endure, their policy is to attack by every means possible. This has been their motivating force throughout the history of Ireland, ever since Rory O'Moore established "The Defenders" in County Kildare in 1565. At that time priests were being hunted and executed and Catholics were liable to severe sanctions for practising their religion. The Defenders formed a guard to protect anyone in danger of being prosecuted. I must add that many of our greatest leaders among the various militant societies have been Protestants. Our war is by no means a Catholic against Protestant affair. It is, rather, a matter of Irishmen who want to be free from oppression.

Tim, who is well versed in the history of Ireland, reminded me that a branch of a secret society under Sir Phelim O'Neil joined the Confederation of Kilkenny in 1642. In this organization Lord Gormanstown and Lord Mountgarret led the Catholics in the fight for freedom. These groups gradually disappeared though for a long time they defended farmers and labourers against the rapacious instincts of the landlords. In later years their work was more of a pacific nature. But what good any kind of movement in defense of our rights can accomplish today is, in my mind, very questionable.

Tim protests vigorously against the sight of hungry men loading golden corn and grain and choice meat products onto conveyances that transfer it either to the well-stocked and well-guarded granaries of the landlords or to shipping docks whence it is sent to England.

There is hardly any suffering comparable to the gnawing pangs of hunger. Though I am much better off than the average tenant on this estate I am never entirely free of the ravages of hunger. And I can imagine what it is like when it finally saps the energy to such a degree that death becomes a welcome deliverer.

February 24. After Mass on Sunday the proctor got up on a stone in front of the Church and announced that the landlord had kindly taken the desperate situation of the people into consideration. He read a letter addressed to the tenants of this estate. Supposedly it was from the landlord but that is very unlikely for he hasn't been seen in Ireland for well over a year. It is likely from the agent who is well trained in bleeding everything he can out of the human and the material resources on the estate. As nearly as I can recall the message of the letter was the following:

> There is no hope for you as long as you remain in Ireland. The only means of improving your situation is to leave the country. All those who are in arrears for rent will be forgiven what is due, passage to Canada will be paid and you will be given a title to free land from our agents in Canada.

The message raised a flicker of hope in the hearts of many though they doubted the agent's authority to issue it. People gathered in groups and discussed it at length. The general conclusion seemed to be that anything would be better than conditions in Ireland at this time, even if it meant facing the unknown.

There was hardly a single person at Church today who had not lost one or more family members or near relatives from the plague. We didn't think it was possible for things to get worse but they are. Typhoid and dysentery have now become an epidemic. Starvation makes people easy victims of both the fever and the dysentery. What I heard today convinces me that I will have to close the school.

I must add a personal note here. It is a very dark cloud that has no trace of a silver lining. In spite of the dejection I feel over the state of affairs I was immeasurably uplifted, even thrilled, by the beautiful voice of Eileen Shanahan who sang two hymns during Mass yesterday. Her voice was unusually spirited and vibrant and I felt that she was making a special effort to lift the spirits of the forlorn-looking congregation.

Eileen and I are engaged but the very thought of marriage, with plague and famine haunting us at every turn, is nothing short of ridiculous.

February 26. I gave the children the week off. My excuse was that I would be away for a few days. While it is true that I intend to travel a bit I really wanted to break them in gradually for a final dismissal.

A visit to the Connemara and Galway districts confirmed what Tim Maloney told me about the incredible intensity of suffering all along the west coast. This is an area where, I thought, the possibility of adding fish to the meagre food rations might stem the tide of human suffering. Thousands are dying in a state of total abandonment, without even the luxury of a burial trench. Some have been found dead with grass in their mouth. Dogs and donkeys have become common items of diet. Scores of bodies lie along the roadsides and in abandoned

With doubt thrown on the landlord's good faith, the poor people went on arguing among themselves, until a majority decided to stand out and demand better terms. On hearing this, the agent sent word they must decide within a week. If they rejected the offer, it would be withdrawn and no new one would be submitted. My uncle had come to get my advice, "For sure," he said, "you are the only scholard in the family." I comprehended the infamous nature of the offer. The people did not own the land, but they owned the improvements they had made on it, and had a right to be compensated for them. I knew my uncle when a boy had rented a piece of worthless bog and by the labor of himself, and afterwards of his wife, and children, had converted it into a profitable field. Should I advise him to give it up for a receipt for back rent and a free passage to Canada? I tried to find out what he thought himself. Are you for accepting the offer, uncle?

"That depinds," he answered. "Give me a crop of spuds such as we had in the ould times, an niver a step wad I muv."

From the original journal

shielings where they are a prey to the rodents.

I made many inquiries about the planned emigration to Canada and it seems to be well established that the landlords have banded together to come up with this plan to rid their estate of the poverty-stricken, half-starved tenants whom they look upon merely as an encumbrance. Now that the people are without resources and have no strength to till the land they are no longer useful to their overlords. They plan to bring in Scottish sheepherders to occupy the vacated territories and make them yield revenue once again.

February 28. Encouraged by Tim Maloney and his supporters many are now in favour of holding out for better terms from the agent. On hearing about this the agent published another message telling them they had to decide within a week to accept the terms already offered. If they refuse he warned them that no new offer would be made. The infamous nature of the deal is now becoming clear.

The tenants are not allowed to own the land they live on but their little holdings are an intimate part of their very existence. This is particularly true in regard to the poor. In their search for a bit of security they cling to whatever little share of earthly goods they can claim. The land and the humble dwellings they live in bear the marks of years of struggle entailed in improvements that have to be given up now in exchange for a doubtful offer.

The leaders of the Young Ireland group are all for ignoring what they see as a crooked deal. A surprisingly large number of younger men have joined them. While I admire their sincerity, I fail to see how they can accomplish anything with neither guns nor food at their disposal. Perhaps there is an important element of survival inherent in the very act of defying those who are trying to destroy us.

On my short trip down the west coast I got a copy of the London *Times*. It is very plain that the *Times* is directing public opinion against us. In both editorials and news items the Irish people are being blamed for the disastrous state of the country. No mention is being made of the real perpetrators of the schemes that have brought us to this low level of existence. One particular news item about Ireland caught my eye. It was a terse account of a solution that the British Parliament, after long deliberation, has apparently come up with, to relieve the hunger stricken masses in Ireland. The plan is based on the principle that "some means must be found in Ireland" for the relief of the distress. The means that should be employed are transparently visible to anyone who knows our situation. First of all, instead of shipping food out of our country it should be left here for the hungry. In the second place the hundreds of thousands of acres of land that is under full control of the landlords should be returned to its rightful owners, the peasants of Ireland. A third measure that should be taken is the removal of thousands of police and militia who are here with the blessing of the British Parliament to execute, imprison or send to exile anybody suspected of a vaguely-defined offence called "treason". It includes such actions as stealing a cob of corn from the landlord's supply.

In spite of this pronouncement by the British Parliament nothing worthwhile will be done. It is a small consolation, however, to know that some of the truth about conditions in Ireland is getting out. The above-mentioned news article states that one member of parliament pronounced the reports about a famine in Ireland as "perfectly illusory".

March 1. In most parts of the west and the south, people are already getting their tickets for Canada and the agents are posting dates of sailing. At the same time some relief measures are beginning to take shape. One plan calls for various kinds of employment with subsistence pay for work done. The trouble is that those who are in the greatest need for relief are hardly able to stand up, let alone engage in physical labour. There are soup kitchens in the working areas but very few Irishmen will "take the soup."

Another kind of relief measure that looks promising is an order for corn from the United States. If we get it in time it may save many lives. We must wait to see if this measure will be effective.

The most heartsome of all the forms of relief that we can think of is the contributions that are starting to come in from many parts of the world. I hope to have some details on these contributions later on in my journal. There are even some local relief grants. Properly administered they could save countless thousands from death by starvation. But I have found out, from reliable sources, that about seventy-five per cent of the allocated funds are ending up in the pockets of greedy, corrupt officials charged with the distribution of the funds. Our enemies are capitalizing even on our hunger.

March 3. I started school after Christmas with 23 pupils. This week there are 14 left. I don't think I can endure facing their pathetic-looking glances much longer. I am trying to teach them something about the various uses of numbers, though about the only practical calculating they can do is to count the number who are dying around them every day. And as far as history is concerned I must gloss over what is too poignant or nostalgic. They have already too many serious ideas in their minds. I teach some Gaelic since it is the language of most of their parents, though officially it is forbidden in the schools. They seem to love poetry so I go over some of our own choice ballads every day. So many of them have the talent and the liking for learning that the thought of closing the school disturbs me very much.

March 7. I rose early this morning and set out in the mist and fog, stepping briskly, for I had a long way to go to Church. I arrived a bit late and, to my surprise and joy, saw a companion and dear friend of my seminary days – I spent two years at Maynooth College – at the altar saying Mass. He is well known in this area, Father Tom O'Hare. In his sermon he showed himself as he always was, bold and strong and right to the point. He lashed out at those who surrendered to their baser instincts, their passion for material goods and for power, bringing untold misery on those who were their victims. He touched on the age-old question, "How can the Providence of God allow such things to happen, such human misery as we are now going through?" He asked us to remember that, despite the Golgotha we are going through, there will be a resurrection and a judgment with redress of all wrongs. He called upon us all, meantime, to do all that the Law of God – which is certainly not the law of this land, he pointed out – permits us to do, to relieve our own misery and that of our neighbour. I know that Father Tom secretly supports the principles of the Young Ireland Movement. This fact, together with his habit of speaking out boldly as he did today, puts him in serious danger. There are informers, generally renegade Catholics, placed in all of our Church congregations. I am sure that today's sermon will be reported before nightfall.

Father Tom noted my presence in Church and he sent an altar boy to ask me to come and see him. After a hearty greeting he led me to his humble presbytery for a cup of tea.

While we were seated at the table a haggard-looking woman came to the door. She was Father Tom's aunt, Mrs Murtagh. He addressed her rather sternly.

"I sent for you, Aunt Kate, to see what you look like after renouncing your Faith for a bowl of soup."

The woman defended herself by saying that in her heart she didn't renounce anything. "The children are starving", she said, "I had to get them something to eat." Father Tom relented, invited her in and gave her a little parcel of food from his almost empty cupboard. After she left I told him that I was surprised to see him take exception to the poor woman's visit to a soup depot. He apologized for his remarks and confessed that it was his utter disgust over the indignities to which the poor people were being subjected by the soup dispensers that moved him to talk that way. He referred to the revolting scenes of proselytizing that he had witnessed. People were given soup on the condition that they renounce the Faith they held and became members of the State Church. On top of all that they were reminded that they were beggars, receiving food from benevolent benefactors to whom they must be very grateful. "Perhaps," he said, "it is better sometimes that the body be destroyed rather than submit to an extinction of the spirit." Father Tom is anything but legalistic, however. I know for a fact, for example, that at the risk of his life he took part in a few raids on landlords' supplies to save people from starvation.

We had a long chat about the emigration movement. We agreed that it would be better to meet death right here, in preference to submitting to the treacherous terms of the landlords.

We did not mention it but I've heard that there is a price on his head. I feel that this will be our last meeting. When told about my engagement to Eileen Shanahan he was genuinely pleased and favoured going ahead with the marriage, suggesting that it would be a small tribute to life in a world of death. If we do get married I hope to have him perform the ceremony. We both realize that

under present conditions, with famine and disease and
oppression all around us, it is impossible to plan the
future. We said goodbye, mindful of the dangers that lie
ahead of us. Father Tom is one of the many priests who
are living constantly among the victims of the grim
reaper, helping them at times to hold onto the fragile
thread of life, anointing them when they reach the end
and trying in general to lift them out of the despair and
sense of hopelessness that is killing as many as the famine.

I will conclude this entry in my journal with a news
item from the *Southern Reporter,* published in Cork. It
was handed to me by Father Tom. It is about a shipload
of provisions outbound for England:

A valuable cargo, borne by the steamer Ajax which
sailed yesterday from Cork, consisted of: 1514 firkins
of butter, 102 casks of pork, 144 hogshead of whiskey,
844 sacks of oats, 247 sacks of wheat, 106 bales of
bacon, 13 bales of ham, 145 casks of porter, 12 sacks of
vetch, 28 bales of feathers, 3 casks of magnesia, 8 sacks
of lard, 296 boxes of eggs, 30 head of cattle, 90 pigs,
220 lambs, 34 calves, 69 miscellaneous packages.

The annual six million pounds of taxes and rental fees
together with tax grants to the State Church, added to a
veritable fleet of merchant vessels laden with the choicest
food products for export, helps to explain why we are a
poverty stricken, starving nation. But the London *Times*
continues to accuse us of being improvident while the
State Church keeps reminding us that the famine and
pestilence are a visitation from Providence.

The Irish were naturally bitter about having to
support the State Church and about being expected to
pay allegiance to it. It is looked upon as a mild form of
treason to belong to any other Church. For centuries

there has been bitterness between the Irish Catholic and the English Protestant. It dates back to the reformation. Ireland alone, among all the nations of Europe, was scarcely influenced by the reformation. This resulted in a kind of religious war. It was one of the reasons for England's desire to bring Ireland to her knees. One of the chief objectives of the Orangemen, a secret society founded in 1795, was to insure the dominance of Protestantism, by recourse to arms if necessary. The Penal laws were basically anti-Catholic laws. While they were in full force no Catholic could vote or sit in parliament; they were excluded from the bar, the university and all public offices. They could not possess arms or a horse. No Catholic could keep a school or have his children educated. Catholic Bishops were banished and liable to be hanged, drawn and quartered if they returned. All kinds of privileges were offered to those who renounced their faith and became Protestants. (J. M.)

Beranger has touched a thousand hearts by the picture of Pauvre Jacques who, when the tax gatherer came in the king's name, was discovered dead on his miserable pallet. But at Skibbereen, in fruitful County Cork, whose seaports were thronged with vessels laden with corn, cattle and butter for England, the rate collector told a more tragic tale. Some houses he found completely deserted. In one cabin the only occupants were three corpses. In a once prosperous home a woman and her three children had lain dead for a week. The place is a mess of disease, famine and death. Poor creatures, trying to live on one feeding a day, were sinking fast. A woman evicted from a rude shelter in which she lived was found dead in a quarry. (Gavan Duffy)

March 8. Evictions and tumblings are going on at a
mad rate now. The tumblings are cruel. The brutality of
the herds of marauders who are smashing down the
humble cottages of the tenants knows no bounds. People
are beaten, even killed, when they resist. They are given
no time to remove their few belongings. Seldom are
there any reasons given for the evictions. Living on a
choice bit of land, not turning in enough crop to the
landlord, being in arrears with the landlord's rent or the
fees collected by the State Church – any of these can
serve as excuses for the tumblers to demolish a cabin
without warning. These things are happening not only
on Lord Palmerston's estate but all throughout western
and southern Ireland. Without shelter or food, exposed
to the inclemency of the weather at this time of the year
they are perishing by the thousands. It is heartbreaking to
see so many little children dying under these conditions.

Where he got it I cannot say but Tim Maloney came
to my lodging this evening with a little jug of poteen. I
always enjoy his visits for he is well-informed. He told
me that he had recently called on one of Ireland's great
patriots, James Clarence Mangan. He claims that Mangan
is near the end of his rope. Between general ill health and
his habit of drowning his sorrows in the bottle, he is a
very sick man. But he continues to pour out his soul in
song. With great feeling Tim recited all of Mangan's
Dark Rosaleen. This is the name Mangan chose to
represent Ireland in her sorrows. It is forbidden by law to
use it. Severe penalties are meted out to anyone guilty of
either writing or uttering the expression. This merely
inspired Tim to recite with greater zest.

As usual we got talking about some of the historical
precedents to what is going on today in Ireland. The
tumblings and evictions that we are witnessing are
patterned on the barbarous Gerrard evictions. Not so
long ago several hundred fairly comfortable families in

Ballinglass, Galway, were living on a stretch of land that they had reclaimed and improved by dint of hard labour. Without any warning a horde of marauders descended upon them, drove them out of their homes and destroyed all buildings and furniture. Clutching to what few things they could carry with them, the women and children ran into hiding in the ditches along the roadway while the outraged men tried to make a last stand. But the eviction squad was well armed and several of the men were shot down. The survivors built shelters along the roadway but these too were smashed to the ground as soon as they were discovered. Tim's brother was among those who were killed.

We asked ourselves what could possibly have stirred up such fiendish behaviour among people who are supposed to be civilized. Part of the answer, we agreed, lies in the fact that most of the so-called custodians of the law and other kinds of enforcement officers that England has sent over here, belong to the lowest dregs of English society. In fact many are released prisoners. They are joined by a contingent of traitors from our own country. If we add to this the indignation that the landlords and the occupying troops feel over our habit of refusing to accept the yoke of foreign domination, of giving vent to our intense love of freedom and of our land, we can understand the fury of our enemies.

Tim maintains that ever since Cromwell's butchery of every man, woman and child in Drogheda centuries ago, there has never been a time when acts of violence have not been used to suppress our people. Not that we have been free from violence on our side for the secret societies have used both guns and pitchforks in their attempts to strike back. But we never descended to the level of the savage, brutal tactics of our enemies.

We have recent news from Skibbereen and things are very bad there. It's the Gerrard evictions story almost to the letter. Until very recently Skibbereen was a well populated, relatively prosperous district. Today there is nothing but death and destruction in the whole area. In cottages still partly standing, bodies are lying where death claimed them. Most of the homes have been razed to the ground. It seems that a police unit, hand picked for their brutality, led a squad of ruffians into the district where they gave full vent to their lower instincts.

We scanned a recent issue of the London *Times*. It was a pleasant surprise to see a news item which admitted that things are not perfectly normal in Ireland. Some news of famine and the atrocities must be getting out. One member of parliament has, apparently, expressed his disapproval of the despicable operations of agents of the Crown here. If we can only get the truth about our situation to reach the outside world we would receive both moral and material help. The people of England would surely come to our rescue if they were informed of our plight. Tim doesn't believe this. He is convinced of the existence of a plan, now in progress, calling for the destruction of the Irish nation.

March 9. I had a long chat with Eileen today. She came to the school and saw my woe-begone little group of scholars. Acutely aware as she is, of all that is going on, she still continues to radiate happiness. On the way home she expressed her complete agreement with my plan to close the school very soon.

The main topic of our conversation was the emigration movement. Should we join the emigrants or should we stay here? We both want to do something for our people and the choice is a difficult one to make. The vast majority of the tenants in this district have made the decision to risk emigration. They are our kith and kin. And once they sign a paper they will be at the mercy of the landlords and their agents. We feel that they are the ones who will be in great need for help. These considerations make us feel that we should join them. Eileen's father, the last of her family, is going to move to Limerick where some of his relatives live. He is in ill-health and feels that his term is short.

When I began this journal it was my intention to write down the facts even though they may sound depressing and even exaggerated. But I say again, on my word of honour, that what I am writing is far from any exaggeration. As a matter of fact I feel frustrated by my inability to find words that can adequately describe the desolation and destruction that is so widespread.

All along the west coast, particularly in Galway and Connemara, the fishermen sold everything they owned last year in a desperate attempt to buy food for their families with the result that now they have no equipment for fishing. The families of the countless thousands of policemen, land agents and other officials who have been sent to Ireland to enforce the unjust laws that have been imposed upon us, are the beneficiaries of the little belongings that our people often sell in an attempt to survive. Those who officially declare themselves members of the State Church are well supplied with food and protection.

Eileen tells me that the workhouses are filled to capacity all over the southern and western regions. It shows how desperate the people are when they even think of entering these hellish places of refuge. Many are escaping after a taste of what it means to live in them. The main item of diet is a watery cabbage soup and some kind of hardtack resembling sea biscuits. The worst feature of all poorhouses is the frequent lectures, by agents of the Crown, on the impropriety of beggars showing any signs of ingratitude for the favours they are receiving. No consideration is given to those who wish to enter with children, husband or wife or parents. In fact the agents seem to consider it their duty to separate family members, for what reason I cannot fathom.

We make a habit of gathering news, both by word of mouth and from the printed word, always hoping that the tide will turn. Often what we hear merely reinforces our feelings of frustration. Eileen showed me a clipping from the London *Times* which shows how ridiculously ill-informed, or should I say deliberately blind, are the people who are mainly responsible for our condition. The clipping contained a news item which tells us that the Queen, on the basis of information given to her by ministers of the government, declared that there seems to be a "dearth of provisions in Ireland". If she had only declared that there is a "dearth of provisions for a few million who are under the heel of oppression and plenty of food for the chosen few," she would have been telling the truth. It is likely too that the Queen's palace and the homes of the lords of parliament are well stocked with the choicest of food shipped from this country.

In fruitful County Cork, whose seaports are thronged with vessels laden with food for England, the rate collector told a tragic tale. In some houses he found corpses of a whole family, dead for some time. Some houses were completely deserted. Along the ditches were bodies badly mangled by animals. The poor creatures who were still alive were walking ghosts. Any peasant in that area who accepted any kind of relief had to forfeit his holdings. In the southwest a small group revolted. Eleven were hanged. To lie down and die like cattle in a murrain seemed to be the inevitable fate of most. Two little boys, aged twelve and fourteen, were ordered transported to Australia for seven years for stealing some corn. Hearing these things about our own people makes it hard to preserve the sober use of reason. After relating the above details to Eileen I remarked that she was visibly shaken so I resolved to change the topic of conversation to something less disheartening. But she told me that she had heard of things just as bad in the Westport area. She is very anxious that I continue my journal and lends her support by saving news items for me. The following is a quotation from one that she handed to me this evening.

The town of Westport has become a strange and fearful sight. Its streets are crowded with gaunt wanderers, shuffling to and fro with a hopeless air and a hunger-stricken look. A mob of starved, almost naked women surrounded the poorhouse asking for soup tickets. Some are seemingly able to stay alive only as a result of a long apprenticeship to want and through the touching charity which prompts the Irish peasant to share the little he has with someone who is more needy. In Claddagh the fishermen have sold all their nets and tackle to buy soup and corn. When the herring shoals approached the coast they were helpless. It is becoming a common practice to steal something so as to be sent to jail where it might be possible to stay alive.

It seems that over ninety per cent of the people in that district are either dead or in the poorhouses. And this is a region where about forty thousand pounds was collected annually from the tenants.

In spite of our acute awareness of all that is taking place Eileen and I once again spoke of our engagement. She is in favour of our getting married in the very near future since, if we join the emigrants, there will be little time left before departure. I agree heartily. We will try to get in touch with Father Tom O'Hare.

March 10. Strange as it may seem, the Young Ireland Movement is rapidly gaining ground. There is no shortage of recruits. What puzzles me is the reason for their apparent immunity to arrest. Tim Maloney who is about as sharp-witted as anyone I know, appears to have the explanation. When I brought up the question this evening he came out with one of his rather frequent little verbal explosions in Gaelic. "T'anam 'on diabhail, 'amadán!" He is liable to call anyone who is not up to him an amadán. "Sure it's a repetition of the diabolical scheme devised by Pitt in 1798" he said. I should have thought of it myself. It was the year of the uprising that was secretly instigated and promoted by Pitt himself. When the organization was complete and ready to strike, the leaders were all captured and sentenced to be hanged. Pitt's successors are now working on a similar scheme. Tim and other patriots like him are trying to warn the Young Ireland group. News has leaked out that England intends to add twenty thousand troops to the already formidable number billeted in Ireland. As might be expected, the London *Times* is editorializing on the ingratitude and the rebellious nature of those of us who dare to express any kind of opposition to the forces that are crushing the life out of us.

It strikes me that, in the rebellion of 1798 and in every uprising of its kind, Ireland lost many of her most distinguished citizens. They were invariably executed or deported without any semblance of a fair trial. Most of them were noted scholars, outstanding statesmen and men of good moral character. It is ironical that those who executed sentence upon them were, in general, their inferiors in every way, apart from their ability to use brute force. I am thinking particularly of leaders like Lord Fitzgerald who sacrificed his life fighting for our rights. Betrayed by an informer he was imprisoned and subjected to subtle forms of torture which brought on his death. I have among my papers the notice of his death, forwarded to his wife, Lady Connolly. Here is a copy of the note. I enter it here in memory of him and of all those like him who were executed or banished.

Newgate Prison. 6 o'clock, June the third, 1798. Mr Garnet presents his most respectful compliments to Lady Louise Connolly and begs leave to communicate to her the melancholy intelligence of Lord Edward Fitzgerald's death. He drew his last breath at two o'clock this morning . . .

On being refused permission to be with him at the end, his brother, Lord Henry Fitzgerald, exclaimed to the officer in charge of the guard: "You have murdered my brother amongst you as surely as if you had put a pistol to his head."

The leaders of the Young Ireland rebellion, among whom are some of my most respected friends, will surely meet a similar fate.

March 11. Tomorrow is Thursday, the day I intend to close my school. The board members are not at all averse to closing all the schools in the district. Those among them who are not on our side, the side of the poor and of those who do not belong to the State Church, begrudge our people an education. Not so long ago it was a criminal act for anyone to try to get an education. My own father, a hedge schoolmaster, lived in those times. He had his little groups of scholars trained to scatter and hide in the hedges and bushes when the hounds of the law were known to be tracking him. Fortunately he never became the victim of an informer.

I am packing my few books this evening and trying to brace myself for tomorrow. Eileen knows the way I feel about it all and she is coming to visit me tomorrow evening. We will make our final decision on the emigration question.

March 12. I sat at my desk in school for a long time

after the children left today. It was with tears in my eyes
that I told them they would have to stay home for a
while, though I myself knew it was forever. The ordeal
of witnessing them trying to say goodbye to me was
crushing. Some of them seemed to know that it was a
final goodbye. The extreme passiveness that was their
usual attitude towards life and its contingencies in
general, a passiveness that is caused by hunger and other
sufferings, seemed to give way to a flood of mixed
emotions expressed in their tearful farewells. I myself was
more deeply moved than any of them. I never realized
that I loved them so much. Perhaps it was because I
realized that it was the only balm I could administer to
them in their sorrow. What will happen to them now?
Many will soon be dead from hunger and disease.
Perhaps a few will be with us on the boat to Canada.

After dismissal I spent a long time gazing at the empty
benches, unable to move. I have often had the feeling of
a lump in my throat but the intense feeling of loneliness
that overcame me there at my desk surpassed anything of
its kind that I ever went through. Somehow the scene
encompassed the total meaning of Dark Rosaleen's
centuries of suffering. I did not wish to be relieved of the
burden of this loneliness. It was as if I was privileged in
carrying my little share of the sorrows of my people.

The ordeal must have affected me deeply for when I
came to my boarding house, Mrs Moriarty was concerned about my well-being. She even asked me if I
might have a touch of the fever. She went to extra pains
to prepare some broth for my supper. She herself was, in
fact, deeply disturbed over my having to close the school.

Eileen arrived early and, to get our minds off the
present, we talked about our immediate future. If we are
to join our people in their exodus we must get things
done immediately. March 25 is our choice for a wedding
date. Getting our few belongings together will be a

simple matter for we own very little of this world's goods.

I am wondering, as I continue these entries in my journal, whether or not there are too many personal references in it. I trust that if it ever gets out to the public these personal things will be interpreted as relating to what is happening in general rather than just to myself.

I was not at all surprised when Tim Maloney dropped in this evening. He keeps steady on the move and is finely tuned to what is really happening in these dark times. As usual he brought some important news. Referring to the emigrants he told us that the landlords have selected the old, the infirm, the children and the destitute for the first shiploads to Canada. Anyone who is still able to work for them, to make the land produce, they are trying to hold back.

Tim's second piece of news was about the imported corn. Shiploads have already arrived from the United States. Some of it has been distributed. It is a flint-cored variety, quite different from the soft, appetizing type grown here. A lot of elderly people and children have contracted a violent kind of dysentery after eating it. Now they are giving out instructions on the method of cooking it to make it edible. Even if the instructions do reach the people, those who need it most will likely be unable to prepare it since they need cooking utensils and a fire which a great many do not have. No matter what they do with it everybody knows that as a sole item of diet it is almost useless. The empty stomachs of those weakened by hunger cannot hold it.

The third report Tim brought us was a startling one. It is a story of incredible trickery. The British have sent a delegation to Rome where they succeeded in convincing the Pope, who undoubtedly knows nothing about the crisis here in Ireland, that we are a nation of secret societies, engaged in revolutionary tactics and in revolt against the laws of the land. As a result of this latest act of effrontery all of us who make any move that our oppressors can translate as revolutionary are liable to excommunication. The most shocking feature of this intervention is the fact that England has a law which forbids her from having any contact with Rome. It is reminiscent of the false testimony that resulted, a long time ago, in Rome sending aid to King William's forces at the Battle of the Boyne. Though we cannot credit our enemies with intelligence or wisdom we must never underestimate their cunning.

As if to complete the above picture, Her Majesty's Government has just passed a new Treasons Act making it an offense punishable by death or life imprisonment for any of us to hold a meeting under any pretext whatsoever, apart from public worship once a week and conducting approved schools.

In the case of public worship a government official is to be present to censor all proceedings. To those of us who know the history of our country this is nothing new. There have been many such acts during the centuries of occupation. Besides forbidding assembly the act contains sanctions covering words and deeds that local agents of the Crown may classify as treasonable according to their judgement. The passing of this act will surely be followed by orgies of executions and imprisonments. For a meeting such as we were holding here tonight we could reap the full penalties of the new act.

I tried to convince Tim that the odds against fighting back are too great, that the patriotic groups don't stand a chance. But he has all the ardour and inner strength of a man who is fighting, not so much against odds, as for a cause and I know that he would prefer to die on the field of battle rather than surrender. When I suggested that we limit our resistance to a war of ideas he reminded me that it was forbidden under the Treasons Act to hold any kind of meeting. The penalty was life imprisonment or summary execution. He named many of Ireland's most gifted leaders who paid the supreme penalty for their attempts to remove the injustices that plague us at every turn.

I said goodbye to Tim tonight with the strange feeling that we would not meet again. He does not try to cover his tracks and the enemy must surely have him marked by now. We seem to be always cursed by the presence of informers who are ready to betray us for some paltry privileges even though they know that they must leave the country once their treachery is found out.

2

Too Little, Too Late

In the 1840s, after nearly seven hundred years of attempted domination by England, Irish poverty and misery appalled the visitor to Ireland. All this wretchedness and misery could, almost without exception, be traced to the system under which land was occupied, mostly by foreigners. The terms under which the peasant occupied the land were harsh. The majority were tenants 'at will', meaning at the will of the landlord. He could turn them out whenever he chose. The peasant was thus deprived of all initiative and security.

(Atlantic Monthly)

March 13. The outside world is finally learning about our plight. Contributions are coming in. Newspapers in Dublin and Cork are publishing the names of countries, all over the world, that are collecting money and sending it here to help provide food for the starving. This is very uplifting. The thought that the outside world is concerned about us adds hope where all is despair. This concern will surely bear fruit. It is important that the word gets around to the people here. So many have abandoned all hope. News like this should help to put some spirit back into their wasted bodies. I got most of the following information from the *Cork Examiner*.

The Sultan of Turkey was among the first to send us a donation. The working people of England took up substantial collections to help us out. We even have friends among some of the politicians in England as well as among the nobility. The Czar of Russia, the Emperor of China and local potentates in Egypt and India have also sent funds for our relief. Some of these nations are looked upon as socially and culturally inferior to western nations in general and yet in this critical situation, where human rights and human dignity are being trampled upon, they are the first to take action. Those who assume the right to set the standards for cultural and social superiority appear to need further education on the real meaning of these terms.

The United States, the chosen homeland of many thousands of Irish emigrants, outdid all others in generosity. A city named Philadelphia topped all other United States centres in the magnitude of its donation. The Jewish people of New York City matched the Irish in their response to a public appeal for funds. Among all the donations from various parts of the world there is one that is singularly appreciated. It comes from a small tribe of native North American Indians, the Chocktaw tribe from central western United States. These noble-minded people, sometimes called savages by those who wantonly released death and destruction among them, raised money from their meagre resources to help the starving in this country. This is indeed the most touching of all the acts of generosity that our condition has inspired among the nations.

March 14. A riot occurred in Limerick yesterday. Some

of the Young Ireland group attacked a food convoy on the way to a loading port. Hundreds of troops marched on them and beat them unmercifully. Many were shot down. The rest were taken prisoners and that will be the end of them. Tim Maloney has finally been arrested. Needless to say there will be no trial. He will probably be sent in chains to Australia, if he is not executed here.

I visited one of the soup depots this afternoon. The tactics of the soup dispensers were so vulgar that I became both angry and depressed. The haggard-looking women and children in the line-up were reminded, in strident terms, that they were beggars about to receive food through the charity of loyal subjects of the Crown. On hearing this a number of them walked away. Those who remained were given further reminders of how they were to behave. Anybody who attended public worship in a Church other than the State Church was not entitled to charity.

March 15. I read a public auction notice published in the village today. It is not the first one I have seen but since it related to people I know well, people whose children attended my school, it stirred my interest. Here is what was posted, exactly as it was written:

To be soaled by publick cant the 25th inst one pit the property of widow scott one petty coate and one apron the property of widow galaher scazed under and by virtu of an order for the tythe due to Rev. John Bootsides.

The reverend gentleman mentioned has a church capable of seating 400 and he has only 13 families listed as his congregation. In this same area there are several hundred men seeking relief employment on a wage of two pence a day. The clergy are given the right to collect up to twenty per cent in tithes after the landlord bleeds the tenants for rent.

The tenant on a landlord's estate is at the bottom of the economic ladder in Ireland today. If he is fortunate his annual income amounts to six pounds a year. The landlord collects over half of this for rent. The tenant, or cottier as he is sometimes called, ends up with a little over two pounds a year to spend. Slightly above the cottier is the peasant who gets to own a cabin and a small lot. His right to possession rests on his ability to raise money, to the last farthing, for the annual rent. The amount of his rent depends on the arbitrary decision of the agent. He can be dispossessed without notice for any outward expression of what might be interpreted as disloyalty to the Crown. When times are good he can add a turnip and a herring to his daily ration of potatoes. I am speaking of conditions before the famine. Now there is no guarantee of any income or of anything to eat.

There is an increase in the activity of the tumbling squads. Evictions are becoming a matter of course. The roadsides are dotted with the rude shelters of the hundreds who have been driven from their dwellings. This is the way of life here in Sligo. It is difficult to imagine worse conditions but news from other areas south of here is very bad. For many there isn't even a roadside shelter to go to.

There are some tenants who have been in a somewhat more secure position. Eileen's father, for example, had five acres of land and a fairly decent house to live in. People in this class are able to put a little money aside to buy some bread and meat occasionally. But this relative opulence is no guarantee of protection against being evicted. An excuse can easily be found by the agents of the Crown.

I am much interested by what I might call a trait of

character of the suffering masses in Ireland today. In spite of the intensity of their sufferings I have never heard anyone express resentfulness against Providence. They apparently realize, intuitively and by observation, that it is the free will of unprincipled, evil-minded men, rather than Divine intervention, that has ruined our country. Clergy who minister to the dying claim that even in deplorable conditions the people often display a kind of triumphant resignation and peace that is intelligible only on a spiritual plane. Whether in the living or the dying, this indomitable spirit that faces all odds with equanimity might eventually save us from extermination.

In a copy of a November issue of a Dublin paper I read about a visit Lord Russel made to Ireland. The article says that he was impressed by the huge stacks of corn that had been harvested in various parts of Ireland. With the failure of the potato crop he naturally concluded that the people could very well survive on the corn, and that it would not be exported as usual. On hearing this the hopes of the poor were raised. But their optimism was short-lived. Apart from what the landlords kept, the whole crop last fall was exported. Mitchell quoted the case of a ship captain who saw a vessel laden with Irish corn in a South American port at the beginning of December.

March 16. With all the time at my disposal I am giving more attention to my journal these days. This afternoon I visited Uncle Jeremiah. I was surprised to see a goodly stack of corn in the haggard beside his cottage. He told me that the agent was waiting on the price to go up before collecting it all. The size and location of every stack is registered and there are severe penalties for anyone who dares to touch any of it. One of his neighbours was evicted a few days ago for trying to get away with some for his starving family. The mother of the family, Mrs Mick Coady, was dying so the priest was called. When he arrived at the cabin he found the eviction squad at work smashing down the walls with no regard whatsoever for the dying woman. Her husband was trying to move her after getting the five children out into the open. The priest had to plead with the leader of the squad to be allowed to give the woman the last rites before moving her. They continued their depredations while he ministered to her. She died about an hour later within sight of her ruined home. Eileen spent all day yesterday with the children. This is not an isolated case. Similar things are happening all over the country.

I am beginning to get concerned over the increasing indifference with which I am reacting to scenes like the above. A short while ago it would have brought tears to my eyes. It is not that I don't feel very deeply moved. But we can become so overwhelmed by tragedy, I suppose, that we do not respond with the ordinary manifestations of grief. That is, I believe, what is happening to the people in general. We all realize how tenuous is our existence in a land where human life appears to be worth less than that of the beast in the field. Those who evaluate human life in this way, our enemies I mean, must indeed be on the brink of internal decay despite their vaunted material prosperity. I read from an author whose name I cannot recall, a prescribed author in my seminary studies, that the final stage of decay of a nation or people is reached when they cease to respect life and liberty among all humankind.

March 18. A violent form of dysentery has combined with the pestilence and hunger to increase the rate of mortality dramatically. In their vain attempts to save the little ones, mothers are feeding them whatever they can find and often it is indigestible and irritating.

Children have lost their normal youthful appearance.

They look like old people. They do not laugh and play any more. The single ration of soup they get daily isn't enough to put energy into their bodies. In fact some do not have the energy to walk to the soup depot. All are marked for export but it looks as if there will not be many of them left by the time the ships are supposed to leave.

It is pleasant to be able to write something less depressing than my usual entries in this journal. I heard today that in the Galway region one of the landlords lost everything he owned in a heroic effort to relieve the sufferings of his tenants. He is now seriously, perhaps fatally, ill with the fever. His example is a shining light in this hour of darkness. If only some others among the landlords would follow his example, in giving the people the produce from their land and cancelling the rent, a great many lives would be saved.

The emigration scheme, though fraudulent and treacherous, is serving one useful purpose. It is raising a flicker of hope in the hearts of many who would otherwise give up. Countless thousands are now ready to take the chance. In fact there will be a veritable tidal wave of departures. The agents are rushing things more than ever these days. Today the local agent came with an attorney who got the people to sign a paper. I approached the agent and protested against his trying to get them to sign a document which had not been explained to them. It is a legal document with a lot of fine print. The agent refused to discuss the matter. Whether they understand the document or not makes very little difference to the people anyhow, for they must sign or be driven out onto the roads. What they are signing is a release of all claims on their property and furniture and a promise to give the agent possession by April 10. There is no mention of the ten shillings they are supposed to receive on arrival in Canada. Neither is there any mention of the land they are to receive according to the first notice sent out. Nothing can be done about these things now. The people are at the mercy of the landlords.

Eileen and I are looking forward to the date set for our wedding. We have been unable to get in touch with Father O'Hare and we fear that something has happened to him. There could hardly be a more unsuitable time for a wedding but we know that soon we will be on our way to Canada. Perhaps there is little we can do but the emigrants are so much at the mercy of those who are expelling them that we hope to be of some help. When I think of it, this district will be very lonely and deserted after they leave. It would be as heartbreaking to remain here as it is to leave.

March 20. Next Thursday is to be our wedding day. We will try to make some sort of little celebration out of it for the sake of the people. Eileen is on the lookout for some food and Mrs Moriarty is going to do all she can to help. We'll have a couple of good fiddlers and perhaps the pipes to cheer up our guests. It will be perhaps a final party for the neighbourhood before they all begin the long journey to Dublin where they will likely embark.

Father O'Hare's successor here is Father Dan Flynn. He was visibly surprised when we mentioned our wedding date to him. But when he realized that we are all badly in need of something to help us forget our troubles he was eager to do his part and to help out with the little festivities. He told us that informers, hired by agents of the Crown, made a list of complaints against Father O'Hare. These were forwarded to the Bishop who was given the choice of sending him out of the country or having him imprisoned and tried for treason. He is probably in Europe.

We are very much afraid that Eileen's father may be

fatally ill. He took the fever and it may be the end of him. We are going to visit him tomorrow.

March 22. Patrick Michael Shanahan, Eileen's father, died during the night. Like myself Eileen is an orphan now. On account of the pestilence Patrick will have to be buried without delay. We are arranging for the burial tomorrow morning. In a way it is fortunate that he died before our departure as it would have been a sore trial for Eileen to leave him. And now we are asking ourselves serious questions about the propriety of a wedding under these circumstances. Patrick was very much in favour of it and it is a pity he did not last a little longer. In our perplexity we intend to discuss the matter with Father Dan Flynn, the young priest who promised to marry us.

March 23. Uncle Jeremiah brought the body of our dear departed on a hand cart to the graveyard this morning. There were just the three of us present as we laid him to rest, thankful that at least we were able to bury him with dignity. Since we could not get a priest we said some prayers, led by Eileen. She intoned a few verses of that most poignant of all the liturgical chants I have ever heard, the Dies Irae. In that little graveyard, on a cold, rainy March morning, the notes of the chant seemed to swell into a requiem, not only for Patrick Shanahan, but for Dark Rosaleen herself in her agony, for the countless thousands of her children who are perishing in indescribable suffering. With a final Requiescat in Pace we sorrowfully left the little graveyard.

March 24. Tomorrow, Thursday, is still a big question mark. As far as we ourselves are concerned, I mean Eileen and myself, there is nothing to prevent us from going ahead with the wedding ceremony. But convention demands a reasonable period of mourning. Moreover, I must think of Eileen's feelings. This takes priority even over the conventions.

I purposely spoke to several of my closest friends to sound out their opinion. They all seem to think that, considering the times in which we live, there would be nothing indelicate about carrying out our plan. Our neighbours have gone to a lot of trouble preparing for a wedding feast. Father Flynn thinks that there is no valid reason for postponing it. Though our friends would understand a postponement we know that they would all be disappointed if it were put back to a later date. We decided this evening to make tomorrow definitely our wedding day. We don't have any fancy clothes but this will not be embarrassing as everybody is in the same predicament. Some of our guests will have nothing but rags to wear.

March 27. Thursday was our big day and it was indeed a big day for our guests. After the wedding Mass, Father Flynn invited all present to a meal at the schoolhouse at noon hour.

Where it all came from I cannot for the life of me imagine but there before us was a huge pot of hot vegetable soup, scones, and even some cakes, fish and gallons of tea. For the children there was a rare treat, a few pots of milk. For the vast majority of those who came it was the first sight of this kind of food that they had in a long time, over a year for some. It soon became evident that we had a problem of overcrowding so the Church basement was opened and another food depot set up there. When word got around scores of late-comers began to arrive. As if by magic the food lasted till all got their hunger satisfied. When the noon meal was finally over, around two o'clock, Mrs Moriarty announced that a lunch would be served around six in the evening and that it would be followed by a dance and a concert. I couldn't

believe that there would be a bite left for an evening
lunch but somehow there was. Some of us were afraid
that the landlord's supplies had been broken into and that
before the evening was over the police would be after
the culprits. But our fears were apparently ungrounded. If
there actually had been any raids on storage supplies they
must have been carried out under perfect cover for it is
practically impossible to do a thing like this without
being caught.

The evening dance and concert were enough to put
the spirit back into all of us. Paddy Dolan, one of the best
pipers in Ireland, outdid himself. Gavan O'Duffy, a well-
known leader in the Young Ireland group, led the fiddlers
who put on a great show. The concert was mainly a
musical affair. Ballads were sung, a few solos were mixed
in and some patriotic poems read or recited. None of us
would have missed any of it for all the world. Eileen and
I were greatly honoured in being the occasion for a
genuine celebration, a joyful interlude in the stressful
lives we lead with death and despair all around us. As if
to remind us all of the grim reality of life as it really is, I
was asked to recite *Dark Rosaleen* to conclude the
celebration. Eileen reminded me that I could be charged
with treason for even voicing the title of the poem but I
felt that there were no informers among the guests so I
did not hesitate. On this note we broke up the party and
it was with heavy hearts that we all went our separate
ways to face a future that held nothing but grim un-
certainties. Though he was unwelcome and uninvited,
one of the agents of the landlord appeared at the end
with some notices reminding us that sailings for Canada
were scheduled to begin next week.

March 28. There was no Church service today. Father
Flynn is down with the fever. It is unfortunate for this is
our last Sunday before leaving to catch a boat. Practically

all the tenants here have signed the papers brought around by the agent so they have sealed their fate. They were told to be in Dublin by the second of April for embarkation. Most of them will have to walk so they will set out tomorrow morning. Only the old, the infirm and small children will be able to ride, as conveyances are very scarce and too expensive for the poor. They will have to sleep at night along the roadways and bring their little bundles containing food and clothing together with a few small pots and pans and utensils. I will not be surprised if we hear of a good number of roadside burials along the way as some are in poor condition for travel. I would like to walk with them but I fear that the stresses of the recent past have taken their toll on Eileen's health so I have engaged a jaunting cart. We intend to leave the day after tomorrow.

This afternoon we helped Uncle Jeremiah's family to make their preparations. The children, Timmy and the two girls, look much better than when we were here last week. Aunt Mary looks drawn and tired but she has a lot of spirit in her frail body. Eileen prepared a box of food for their journey to Dublin. They will leave tomorrow morning.

March 30. We were unable to leave yesterday because our conveyance was held up for repairs. We were thus in a position to help some people who had difficulty getting organized. It is pitiful to watch the final departures, the backward glances at the poor though precious belongings that they must leave behind. The pathetic farewell glances at their humble dwellings brings tears to my eyes. Many have left already, The rest will be hard pressed to reach Dublin in time for embarkation but I am told that they never leave on time. There are delays of a week or more so as to make sure that the vessels have all the passengers they can carry.

3

The Trek to Dublin

Weary men, what reap ye?
Golden corn for the stranger.
What sow ye? Human corpses for the avenger.
Fainting forms, hunger stricken,
What see ye in the offing?
Stately ships to bear our food away,
Amid the stranger's scoffing.
There's a proud array of soldiers,
What do they round your door?
They guard our masters granaries,
From the thin hands of the poor.
(Lady Speranza)

March 31. It is early morning as I write this last note before departing. We now join a huge army forced to leave their native land for the convenience of the rich and the powerful. The heavy morning mist is a fitting curtain for the final scene, the climax, of all our strivings against impossible odds. It is a scene of utter devastation. A line from *Dark Rosaleen* comes to my mind:

Woe and pain, pain and woe
Are your lot both night and noon.

I cannot help but glance back through the pages of our
history to the years when Ireland was a beacon of
learning and faith whose light spread to all parts of
Europe. Her poets, bards and musicians were known and
loved all throughout the land. Her monasteries were
centres of faith and culture, a light to the world. God
grant that those days of glory may some day return to
Dark Rosaleen.

The judgment hour must first be nigh
Ere you can fade, ere you can die,
My Dark Rosaleen.

We expect to leave after our morning tea. Mrs
Moriarty is staying here. I only wish I could thank her as
much as she deserves for her motherly attention to all my
needs while I was boarding with her. I often didn't have
a penny to pay for my keep but that made no difference
to her. In fact she was always embarrassed when I did
make my payments.

This may be the end of my story about our lot here in
my native land. I have tried to describe conditions and
events leading up to this mass emigration movement.
Perhaps it should be called a mass expulsion movement
for the term emigration implies a free choice on the part
of the emigrant. It is true that many eagerly signed the
papers but behind the signing there was nothing but
dishonesty, deception, fraud and wholesale evictions.
Though nothing can ever adequately fill in for the loss of
all that our people hold dear in the land of their birth, we
all hope that in Canada we will at least find liberty and
respect for basic human rights. Yet the people are afraid.
We will still be under the Union Jack.

Eileen has some tea and scones ready so I will pack my journal in our little box and get ready for departure.

April 3. Dublin. We arrived this evening. Our driver jogged along at a steady pace all the way. We stayed overnight in Ardagh, Longford. There was hardly room to drive along most of the roads, there were so many people on the march with their belongings in all sorts of carts and carriages. It was embarrassing for us to drive past them. We saw several casualties, people who succumbed to the strain of the journey. The victims were hastily buried by the roadsides. The elderly and the little children were the first to fall victims to the fatigues of the march. If we had any space at all in our cart we would have given some help to the most afflicted. On the other hand most of them prefer to remain among their own family and other friends and relatives rather than be separated even when it is a matter of life and death.

I think that I have acquired a deeper understanding of the Israelites' long and painful march from their captivity in Egypt to a Promised Land. I have but to look at what is taking place here in my country. During the past two days I have seen a never-ending stream of gaunt, dejected looking, ghost-like figures shuffling along the roads on their way to the nearest harbour where a transport ship is waiting to take them to a distant country. They are the products of centuries of injustices perpetrated upon them and their ancestors. They are second only to food as chief exports from their native land. Along the way they see loads of the finest agricultural products in the world being transported for shipment to England. Many of them see, too, the ruins of ancient castles that were built by their ancestors and sumptuous residences on large estates owned by outsiders. I believe that there is nothing in the history of mankind to compare with this march, this exodus, of what may amount to a hundred thousand people who are obliged to seek an existence in a foreign land.

April 4. We are staying with some friends of Eileen's in Dublin waiting for orders to board our ship. This morning I went to the harbour to make inquiries. According to the word I received we are due to sail tomorrow but there is a mountain of freight on the dock. It will take several days to load it, I am sure, so we will hardly be leaving till some time next week. I made arrangements for a cabin. It turned out to be a cubby hole in the house on the deck. It may be too early to form an opinion of the ship but it looked frightfully dilapidated as I saw it.

I met Uncle Jeremiah and the family on the deck. They were foot-sore and weary after the long walk. There were several hundred people camped on and around the dock waiting for permission to board the ship. Some have already spent two nights in the open exposed to the chilly winds from the bay. The sky looks threatening and I fear that there will be showers tonight.

I decided to approach the captain to explain the situation and to get him to invite the people on board where they would be sheltered from the inclement weather. He curtly told me to go to the agent. I waited for more than an hour outside the immigration office before being allowed to see the inspector. The latter very haughtily ordered me out when I told him the purpose of my coming to see him. According to the information they received before leaving, the passengers were to be on board today. If they have to remain without shelter until the freight is all loaded it will be a severe hardship. Most of them are scantily clad and have very little bedding.

April 5. Dublin has not been spared from the ravages

of hunger and disease. In fact the poorer sections of the city where hunger is more prevalent are as badly off as any of the disaster areas on the west coast. Not far from the dock I walked through one of these areas and I was shocked, even after my experiences on the west coast, to see the depths of misery and neglect to which these poor people are reduced. They are not receiving any help, for those who are in more comfortable circumstances in other parts of the city are mortally afraid of the fever. They know that the poor and above all the emigrants are the main carriers of the pestilence.

I found out that the fever that is killing so many in this country is cholera morbus or Asiatic cholera. It is a severe, malignant type of the disease. It may begin insidiously with bowel upsets leading to two or three weeks of illness. Or it may have a violent onset with vomiting, purging, anuria, pulselessness, severe cramps and a bluish shrunken appearance of the skin, leading to death in twelve to twenty four hours. The uncertainty of who will be struck down next causes great fear and a feeling of helplessness among the populace. This kind of cholera was endemic to India in the eighteenth century. From there it spread westward to Russia, West Germany and England. It was first recognized in the Port of Sutherland, England, on October 31 1831. In a report in a Dublin newspaper containing the above information I was surprised at some of the suggested causes of the disease. Among them are: the influence of the sun and moon, the approach of a comet, exhalations from the bowels of the earth, poisonous air from decaying animal matter, a change in the ethereal fluids in the atmosphere and lastly, what looks like the real cause, contagion. The report was written by a Doctor Drake. Some of the suggested remedies for the cholera are more fantastic than the generally accepted causes of the disease. One of them, for example, is a red flannel belt soaked in turpentine.

But for all we know it might have genuine healing properties.*

Our friends, where we are lodging, feel that we must have lost the use of our senses even to think of joining the emigrants on what they described as the horrors of the ocean voyage. After reading a newspaper description of ocean travel I am inclined to agree with them. Here is part of the description:

> The crossing takes thirty-six to eighty days. The passengers are herded into small crafts, with usually 250 to 500 per boat. Decks are all flush with a caboose on the galley and the cookhouse over the longboat between the fore and the main mast. The longboat, securely lashed, carries food and livestock. There were some provisions that are issued once a week, like oatmeal, cooked by the passengers in a little galley in the waist of the ship. Sleeping quarters are in the low, dark steerage between decks and midship. Ventilation is furnished by a windsail at each hatch. Sanitation, if any, is of the slop jar variety.

The same article mentions that, since sailings are not carried out on a dependable timetable, emigrants generally arrive at the boat dockside prior to sailing and have to maintain themselves as best they can on shore.

According to all that, it looks as if the worst isn't yet over.

April 6. I rose at dawn and told Eileen that I was going to the dock to see how the people fared during the night. In spite of my objections she insisted on coming with me. I was deeply concerned for it rained all night and it looked as though it would continue throughout the day.

*Editor's note: Typhus was the most prevalent disease in 1847. Not cholera.

I need not describe what we saw at the dock. It was heart-rending. Even if our enemies had carefully planned it they could not have designed a more effective final blow to the already desperately disheartened emigrants. Three or four died during the night and were buried in the early morning in shallow graves not far from the dock. One was a little child who died of exposure. There were three priests making the rounds, anointing some and trying to help others get better organized against the severity of the weather. One of them had been on the dock all night.

It was all too much for me so I left Eileen as she moved among the sick and suffering, helping them in many ways. I made straight for the shipping offices. I waited for the first sign of movement there. After what seemed like the longest two or three hours of my life, a clerk from the ship broker's office admitted me. But the broker told me I'd have to bring my complaints to the charterer before anything could be done for the passengers. At the charterer's office they told me that the man in charge was out of town. It was painfully clear that there was no point in trying to get official help.

Back on the dock I met one of the priests who told me that what was going on was common practice during the 1832 emigration as well as during the present one. A few ships had already left and all of them had their sailing dates delayed so as to make sure they were loaded with human ballast for the benefit of the charterer's purse. Sailing dates were thus deliberately advanced, to the discomfort of the passengers. The priest told me that we could expect absolutely no help from any of the officials as the charterers were remorseless in their greed. They did not hesitate to bribe the inspectors so as to be free to defy the government regulations concerning passengers' rights.

April 7. Eileen was very anxious to get to the dock early this morning. She is one of those rare persons whose very presence has some kind of healing effect on the suffering and depressed. She is also an excellent nurse though not specially trained. With her little box of remedies she works wonders among the sick. I am quite certain that the spirits of the whole company on the dock were uplifted this morning by her presence among them. Several fires were lit to warm some food and Paddy Dolan played a few heartsome tunes on the pipes. Though drinking has not been a problem so far, a few men today had more than was good for them. It was long after sundown when we returned to the city. Though they haven't said a word, I know that the people we are staying with are concerned about our mixing in with the crowds and becoming carriers of the cholera. In order to put them at their ease we made an excuse of having to move nearer to the dock. But they pressed us to stay, reminding us that this may be our last night before boarding the ship.

April 8. We left early again today to find out how the people passed the night. We were told that several men tried to get on board last night but they were driven back and one man was brutally kicked by the mate. Once they do get on board they are entitled to food rations so the ship owners see to it that they embark only at the last minute. I ventured to approach the captain to tell him that the people would not ask for rations till sailing time if only they could get shelter on the ship. He told me that he had nothing to say to an informer, referring to my visit to the agent's office. I replied that I would go to higher authorities about the matter. He merely looked at me with utter contempt. He knew that none of the officials would interfere.

Permission has finally been given to board the ship.

We went back for our baggage and bade goodbye to our generous hosts who begged us once again to change our minds about emigrating. Nothing could have stopped us at this point. We still hope to give some kind of support to our unfortunate fellow pilgrims now that they are at the mercy of the shipping agents.

We were hardly settled in our cubby hole on deck when I saw a great crowd of men, women and children approaching the ship. At first I thought they were passengers for another vessel for we already had more than ours could normally accommodate. To my great surprise and consternation they began to climb aboard so that finally there was hardly room to turn on the deck.

A tug pulled up and passed her hawser. Out in the bay a six-oared cutter came alongside and a government inspector leaped on board. He looked neither right nor left but went straight for the Captain's quarters. I resolved to protest to him against the blatant violation of regulations that restrict the number of passengers according to the capacity of the ship. I waited till he was leaving and approached him. To judge by the aroma that greeted my nostrils he must have been refreshed with a stiff ration of liquor. I got as far as the words "I protest" when I was tripped from behind by one of the ship's officers. As I fell I heard the inspector say, "Poor fellow, he must have had a drop too much. Goodbye Captain, I wish you a prosperous voyage." When I rose to my feet he was gone and the mate was facing me. "Damn you, try to speak to an outsider again and I'll brain you," he shouted. Mortified and indignant I left the quarter deck. We were moving out into Dublin Bay but suddenly the ship dropped anchor. It was Friday so the crew refused to sail, mindful of one of their pet superstitions. We have yet to say goodbye to Dark Rosaleen. A verse of Mangan's poem expresses my feelings admirably:

I could scale the blue air,
I could plough the high hills,
Oh, I could kneel all night in prayer
To heal your many ills,
Dark Rosaleen

4

The Naparima

After centuries of struggles and sufferings a nation of eight or nine million stands before the civilized world as a mendicant for universal charity Her people are starving while her granaries and warehouses are filled with her own grain and provisions which she is not allowed to touch. The treasuries of the Imperial Government are piled up with heaps of riches, a good portion of which was extracted by armed agents, under threat of eviction, from the people of Ireland.

(Rev. Bernard O'Reilly)

April 9. We sailed at daybreak this morning. Our bark, the Naparima, with estimated accommodation for three hundred, has over five hundred on board. It will indeed be a prosperous voyage for the charterers and the Captain who gets five pounds for each passenger. The Naparima is an ancient tub of a vessel that has reached a ripe old age. Her creaking timbers will be severely tested if we run into rough weather.

After dropping the pilot at Kingstown three days'

rations of sea biscuits were served. They were tough and somewhat mouldy but the people were so famished that they ate them without complaint. Unfortunately almost all of them were consumed the first day.

About half of the passengers had no place to bed down for the night. They tried to rest on bundles and chests on the floor of the steerage quarters. What I have seen today of the Naparima bears out some of the details I have already quoted about the whole system of transporting Irish emigrants. It is not an exaggeration to say that anything that will stay afloat and carry a sizable number of passengers is being put into service. I heard that a lot of the boats were built for Canadian lumber export. Some are dismantled when they reach England so that the structural timbers can be used. Others return to Canada with a human cargo as ballast. They take from six weeks to three months to cross the ocean. The holds are dark, cavernous dungeons fitted with narrow movable bunks for the emigrants. There are no lights, no portholes, and no ventilation except for what fresh air enters from the two hatchways.

The legal allowance is thirty-three inches, in width, for each passenger, but the crowding on the Naparima allows only about half of that. By noon hour today the air was already foul and if fever breaks out I fear for the worst. It is an ideal place for disease to spread. There is absolutely no provision for privacy. I wonder what methods will be used to get rid of refuse of various sorts. One redeeming feature is the freedom to remain up on deck in fine weather. This afternoon the deck was crowded.

Eileen has made our own quarters comfortable in spite of its revolting condition when we first saw it. She has thoughtfully arranged a place where I can write in my journal. We stood out on deck for a long time after the pilot put off at Kingstown. Our eyes were fixed on the land we cherish dearly. We know that we are looking at it for the last time. And we feel that our fellow passengers are sharing the sorrow we feel over the parting.

As we sailed along the east coast of Ireland today we were close enough to see the coastal areas of County Wicklow and County Wexford. At Wicklow Head and Carnsore Point we were very close to land. The crowd on deck are all viewing the landscape in respectful silence, getting a last good look at what is for all of us the dearest place on earth. Now I can understand the crushing feeling of loneliness that seizes the exile and the emigrant as he severs the roots that bind him to his native land. And I know that we Irish experience the pangs of parting more intensely that do most other people. This is perhaps because we have suffered so much. And I'm sure we will be forgiven if we give as an added reason that Ireland is a beautiful country in every respect if only it hadn't been mutilated by our enemies.

I was told that if it is bright enough we will be able to see land at Ardmore Head and that we will possibly see the hills of Kerry. If so that will be our final farewell. But whether we see any more or not we all took leave, forever we know, of our Dark Rosaleen as we embarked at Dublin.

I spoke to one of the deck hands who happens to be a Galway man and asked him to call me if he thought we would be able to see the hills of Kerry. It was a clear night with good visibility so he called me very late at night and there in the distance was the faint outline of Iveragh Mountains. I called Eileen and we stood transfixed in silent contemplation. It was an experience we wouldn't have missed for all the world even though it was painful in some respects. I felt that no matter how far I travelled and what other land would adopt me, my heartstrings would always be woven into the land of my birth. Finally the hills of Kerry faded out of sight. Tearfully and silently we returned to our cabin where I sat up long enough to put this entry in the journal.

April 10. Early this evening we began to face a rising wind and a choppy sea. The Naparima began to sway and roll and sea water flooded the deck. The passengers were sealed below, the hatches having been battened. We were getting our first experience of the violent moods of the Atlantic. I convinced Eileen to remain in the cabin while I opened a small hatch above a stairway and descended to the hold. Three blinking lanterns, which someone must have installed since we left Dublin, gave enough light to make out the ghostly forms of the hundreds of passengers in various stages of trying to bed down in bunks or on the floor. The rolling and creaking of the ship in the storm was frightening. The stench from refuse and excreta was nauseating. I wondered how the people could possibly survive six or eight weeks when it was this bad after about two days.

Some were very sick. I found Aunt Mary and the two girls crowded into one bunk while Jeremiah and Timmy were lying on the floor. Some water had trickled in and if things get any worse there could be an emergency. I waited for some time, giving a hand to those who were having difficulty getting a place to lie down. Since the situation didn't appear to be getting any worse I went back above. The hatches are generally fastened down from above for the night but there is a small emergency cover that is left open, allowing me to escape. Eileen, completely exhausted, was asleep so I sat down and entered this note in my journal. As anyone can tell by the writing it is not easy to continue my entries under these conditions. Instead of extinguishing our little lamp I trimmed it and sat reading the first part of the journal to the accompaniment of the sounds of the storm. The wind finally abated somewhat in the early hours of the morning.

One of our many tacks brought us close to the English coast. It was my first and likely to be my last view of that country. Aileen has made our cabin snug and convenient beyond belief. Her happy disposition causes her to make the best of everything.

19. – The westerly breezes that kept us tacking in the channel gave place, during the night, to a strong east wind, before which the ship is bowling at a fine rate. Passing close to the shore we had a view of the coast from Ardmore to Cape Clear. Aileen sat with me all day, our eyes fixed on the land we loved. Knowing, as it swept past us, it was the last time we would ever gaze upon it, our hearts were too full for speech. Towards evening the ship drew away from it, until the hills of Kerry became so faint that they could hardly be distinguished from the clouds that hovered over them. When I finally turned away my eyes from where I knew the dear old land was, my heart throbbed as if it would burst. Farewell, Erin.

From the original journal

April 11. The weather was calmer today but many of the passengers are sick from the unhealthy air in the hold and from the battering we got during the storm. A large number were able to come up on deck during the day though over a hundred were unable to move. Eileen joined me when I went down to visit the sick and she spent over two hours ministering to them.

I had a long chat with the deck hand from Galway today. His name is Martin Riley. He has made several trips and was full of information about the transport of emigrants. He said that a great many were shipped from ports in Ireland to Liverpool where they were often forbidden to land with the result that they were shuttled back to Ireland. Some made the trip five or six times and were eventually put on ships to Canada. A few ships crossed the ocean directly from Liverpool.

Given a free choice, all of the emigrants would have gone to the United States as they wished to escape from the shadow of the Union Jack. But any boat landing at a United States port had to pass inspection and the ship owners knew that hulks like the Naparima and the others like her could never pass an honest inspection. Emigrants from such countries as Germany and Holland travel on ships that have been properly inspected. They have a reputation for cleanliness, good food and excellent passenger accommodation. Emigrants from these countries have no difficulty getting into the United States.

The only food being served on the Naparima is the sea biscuits. As I mentioned before they show signs of having been in storage for a long time. There is an allowance of tea which is a rare treat for most of the passengers. The drinking water has a disagreeable taste which may come from the containers but I fear that before long it will be unfit to drink. Most of us still have some of the food we brought on board.

April 12. We went through another terrifying experience this afternoon. A bad storm arose. The lashings of the ocean gale wrought havoc down in the hold. People were violently tossed about under the repeated blows of mountainous waves. Driving before the gale, close-reefed, the Naparima pitched and shuddered helplessly and she shed tons of water. Only the strongest and the healthiest survived the storm without suffering bodily harm. The weak and the sick had a painful and frightening time of it. Nothing could stop Eileen from going down below with her medicine box. She found some cases of fever and it may be ship fever. If so we are in for an epidemic. I helped her on her rounds and apart from a few bumps from being pitched by the storm we came through the ordeal fairly well. It is almost impossible to write another word tonight so we will try to get some rest.

April 13. We had a dreadful night last night. Neither of us got any sleep. It is a wonder the Naparima didn't fall apart such was the force of the wind and the waves. We tried to get down to the hold this morning but the emergency hatch seemed to be warped and swollen from the flooding so we couldn't open it. This afternoon the storm abated and the mate ordered the hatches to be opened to let the people come up on deck. The first one up was Uncle Jeremiah. He told us that Aunt Mary was seriously ill. We hurried down into the deathly air and found her with a high fever, racked with pain. Eileen gave her a few drops of laudanum. She appeared to be relieved somewhat. But it was evident that she could never recover in the foul air of the hold. I went to the mate and asked him if we could transfer the sick woman to our cabin. He told us that only the captain could decide and that he left orders for no one to disturb him except in an emergency. I did not believe what the mate said so I dropped the matter as I was already in his bad graces.

We remained below for an hour. The stench and the general appearance of the place was revolting. The seams in the forepeak had opened during the storm and water was flowing in. One old man was lying in a bunk with what looked like several broken ribs from being pitched about last night. It was a case that called for the services of a ship's surgeon. But we found out before leaving Dublin that vessels transporting Irish emigrants ordinarily had no medical attendant on board. It seems that every law protecting the passengers is being ignored.

A ten-year-old girl died during the storm. We wrapped her in some rags, took her up and slipped her body into the ocean with our own silent prayers for the poor little creature. Her mother was unable to come up she was so weak.

On returning below we found Aunt Mary rapidly declining. Delirious, she was muttering things about a garden she used to have years ago. After a long search I found a man with a pannikin of water which he gave to me. It was foul and brackish. He told me that it came directly from the ship's supply. In spite of my bad name with him I resolved to see the Captain about it, since water in that condition could prove fatal to anyone who drank it before it was boiled or otherwise purified. I wanted to tell him too that some passengers had the fever.

I waited some time before I sighted him. He had just stepped from the companion and made a couple of rounds on the poop when I approached. I saw him scowl and make as if to walk away.

"Pardon me, Captain, but do you know that there is fever on board ship."

"You lie," he said. "What do you know about fever?"

"Come down below and see for yourself," I replied.

He reminded me in vigorous terms that he knew his duty and needed no advice.

"In that case why is the steerage so filthy and the water unfit to drink?" I asked.

"Grumbling, eh?" he shouted. "What do you want? Roast beef and plum pudding, I suppose. You beggars are on government allowance. Begone or I'll have you locked up."

Repressing my indignation as much as possible I addressed him again.

"But, Captain, all you have to do is to go and see for yourself. When you see the condition of their quarters down below and the kind of food and water they have, you will surely come to their rescue."

I said this knowing that both the Captain and the crew were mortally afraid of going down below, having sniffed the odours coming through the open hatches and knowing that they must have fever on board. The Captain clenched his fist and raised his right arm as if to strike me. At this stage of our encounter I was not to be intimidated. Facing him squarely I continued to press my point.

"Strike me if you wish," I said, "but remember that you are responsible for down below. Between filth and foul air and brackish water they are at the end of their endurance."

"You vagabond," he exclaimed. If you insinuate that I am mistreating anybody I'll have you thrown overboard. Leave the poop or I will kick you off. I'll have no mutiny on my ship."

Though my intervention looked like a complete failure some action was taken. It wasn't much but it helped. Windsails were rigged at the hatchways this afternoon and before long the air in the hold improved considerably.

April 14. Aunt Mary is holding on with no sign of any

improvement. Jeremiah and the children, Timmy, Ellen and Bridget are doing much better than could be expected.

Emigrant ships rarely have enough crew members to do all the manual work that falls to deck hands. It is common practice to enlist passengers to complement the crew. Since this offers a chance for better food and sleeping quarters there is never a scarcity of volunteers. I already spoke to Martin Riley, the man I met soon after boarding the ship, requesting that he put in a word for my cousin Timmy. I warned him not to mention my name as that would only make the mate turn down the request. Timmy is only fourteen but, given a bit of nourishing food he is capable of performing all the lighter chores. To my delight I saw Timmy up on deck just a few hours later, working with a crew member.

As I already mentioned we have had no serious problem with drinking during the first few days on board but things seem to be changing now. The only crew member who ever dares go down below is the steward. He does so in order to collect sixpence from anyone who will buy a drink. This traffic has resulted in some disorder. It is hard to blame a person for taking a drink to help blot out the awful reality of living in a place that is not fit for beasts to live in. But in the long run alcohol is just an added problem. There have been a few isolated cases of drunkenness. Since the captain and the mate share in the profit on any whiskey that is sold, there is no use calling on them to control the traffic.

April 15. I am pleased now with my decision to continue the journal on the ocean since this is another example of the injustices that seem to be our lot in every phase of our enemies' designs upon us. I am referring to the conditions under which the Irish emigrants are forced to travel. If this story could be brought before the public, the laws would become enforced and we would be able to travel like the emigrants from other countries, with decent accommodation and food. Perhaps I can get the press in Canada to reveal the facts about the traffic in emigrants as well as about what is going on back home.

The hatches were opened again today and many came up on deck. They looked for all the world like spectres coming out of tombs with their ghastly complexions and gaunt, emaciated bodies. Perhaps now that they have survived the battering of the Atlantic in some of her worst moods they may have learned how to keep alive during the weeks to come. But that will depend on how much nourishment they can get.

April 16. The main deck was deserted this morning except for three elderly women. The cabin boy flitted about carrying food to where the crew took their meals. The women watched his movements and when he disappeared on one of his rounds two of them hastened to the galley, having seen the cook go to the forecastle. In a twinkling they were out again with a huge copper teapot filled with hot tea. The other woman had meantime gone down to the hold and returned with a lapful of tins of every description. Over the fire which passengers are allowed to build in metal holders on deck, they kept the tea hot. The people below had been warned and were ready for the treat. The tin cups were all filled and refilled and distributed by carriers to anyone who had a taste for it. It was a delightful surprise to all who partook of the treat. When the last drop was emptied they took the pot back to the galley, filled it with water and put it in place. Finally they resumed their seats near the hatch.

By and by the boy returned to the galley. He came back in a few minutes with the cook who had apparently tasted the tea turned into water. Then lightning struck. The mate emerged from the companion and hit the deck with wrathful haste. After hearing the cook's report he threatened to flay the thieves with a rope's end. He approached me and asked what I knew about the whole affair. I replied that I had no hand in it and that, unfortunately, I did not even get a cup of tea. He insisted that I knew the culprits and demanded information. "But," I said, "you have already expressed to me your contempt for informers and now you ask me to assume that role." If Eileen had not been standing by he would have laid me low. He approached the three women and questioned them. I will now give, as near as I can, the words they exchanged.

"Oh it's the tay you're askin' after, mister. Now it wasn't bad at all but a little on the weak side, wasn't it Mrs Finnegan?"

"Yes, indade, but pon me soul it was comfortin', Mrs Dooian. And good it was indade of this fine gintleman to provide for us."

"Who stole the tea kettle?" roared the mate.

"Ooh, my dear, don't be shoutin' so loud. I'm a bit old but not at all deaf as yet. As for the tay kettle sure I saw the boy with it in his hand just this minute."

"I've had enough of your blabber. Who took the tea?"

"Oh, you mean the tay that we are supposed to get every day and for which ten pounds was put down to the mate before we left Ireland. And divil a bit of it have we even tasted till today. Where it's all goin' to I don't know."

"Shame on you Mrs Finnegan for accusing the gintleman of pocketing the ten pounds. You can be sure we'll have it from now on."

The mate was purple with rage.

"You old hags, you know all about this. Show me the thief."

"That's just what we'll do if you'll hold your whisht. Just follow me. It's proud we'll be to have you visit our quarters," said the one addressed as Mrs Finnegan. She beckoned him below. He stood at the hatch with a look of fear and baffled rage. He finally took off towards the poop to the tune of the derisive giggles of the three old ladies. Since the tea belonged to the passengers I had nothing but sympathy for the culprits.

Incidents of this kind are extremely rare, so the little drama was a welcome interlude in the monotony and the hardships of our ocean journey. It took me a long time to finish this note but my enjoyment of the above incident made it a light chore.

April 17. It was the loveliest day so far, a delightful contrast with the terrors of an Atlantic storm. To look at the sails of the Naparima, expanded in a perfect breeze and radiant with the richest tints of the setting sun, you would think that all is well on board. The bounteous displays of nature make it all the more painful to think of the state of the dungeon below decks. We both went down for a visit today and found out that the fever is spreading like wildfire. If the sick only had some nourishing food they could fight fever. They are all becoming indifferent to the punishment they are taking. This loss of hope and even of fear of the physical evil threatening them is the worst feature of their condition. We tried to get as many as possible to go up on deck.

April 18. Aunt Mary died this morning. The deck was crowded as we slipped her body into the Atlantic. I recited some prayers for the dead and Eileen chanted the Our Father. Uncle Jeremiah and the two girls were sad beyond tears. The mate refused permission for Timmy to attend the sad ceremony. We kept the family with us on deck all day.

The outbreak of fever is causing a panic among the passengers and crew. Though we were no strangers to the ravages of the fever back home, we were at least in the open air. To be shut up in a dark dungeon on the ocean racked with fever and pain and facing the prospect of being tossed into the depths of the Atlantic is enough to cause panic even among the most stout-hearted. The mate goes around smelling like a huge bag of camphor. He is mortally afraid of catching the fever and feels that the camphor will protect him. The plaintive cries of those who are delirious can be heard even from the deck.

This afternoon I succeeded in getting a pan of stirabout from the galley for some sick children. You can get almost anything if you are willing to pay enough. As I was on my way to the hold a man sprang suddenly from the hatchway, rushed to the bulwark, his white hair streaming in the wind, and without a moment's hesitation leaped into the seething waters of the Atlantic. His daughter came up to look for him. I led her away gently and handed her over to Eileen but she broke away and continued searching for her father. When the truth finally dawned on her she uttered a piercing cry and rushed to the side of the ship where she scanned the foaming billows. Back in our cabin she collapsed as if dead. Her name is Kathleen O'Shea. Her brother, Gerald, was one of my little group of scholars. He and his mother both died from starvation and dysentery before we left. Kathleen is one more among a multitude of orphans, unfortunate victims of the insatiable greed and the barbarous tactics of our enemies.

April 20. I left my journal aside for a while as I was feeling out of sorts. We are all badly undernourished and the food that we have is not doing us much good. I discovered today that several burials had taken place during the night. The fever is spreading rapidly. I fail to see how any of us can escape it now.

A whale crossed our bow not a hundred yards away this afternoon. The crew takes this seriously. For them it

While I was coming from the galley this afternoon, with a pan of stirabout for some sick children, a man suddenly sprang upwards from the hatchway, rushed to the bulwark, his white hair streaming in the wind, and without a moment's hesitation leaped into the seething waters. He disappeared beneath them at once. His daughter soon came hurrying up the ladder to look for him. She said he had escaped from his bunk during her momentary absence, that he was mad with the fever. When I told her gently as I could that she would never see him again, she could not believe me, thinking he was hiding. Oh the piercing cry that came from her lips when she learned where he had gone; the rush to the vessel's side, and the eager look as she scanned the foaming billows. Aileen led her away; dumb from the sudden stroke yet without a tear.

May 1. – Wind still from northwest; ship beating against it in short tacks. Most disagreeable motion. Cast lead at noon. At 150 fathoms found no bottom. A whale crossed our bows, not a hundred yards away.

From the original journal

portends bad luck, a symbol and a warning of death. Now they are more panicky than ever.

Even though the Captain has it in for me I have to give him credit for being an excellent sailor. Two booms cracked today but that did not deter him from keeping on all the sail he thinks the ship can bear. At times her lee rail almost touches the water. The boatswain claims that we are making record time.

There is a flurry of snow this evening. The weather is very cold and miserable. I counted five bodies being tossed overboard this afternoon.

April 26. I am still under the weather but thank God it isn't the fever. The only events worth noting during the past few days concern the increasing number of casualties, the effects of the severity of the weather, and an unexpected daily ration of tea and soup that the mate has ordered for the people. It is hardly his own promptings that inspired this act of generosity. It is more likely that after our confrontations, he fears being reported when we land in Canada. The Captain must be alarmed over the amount of sickness on board so he may have issued the order. On account of the cold weather there are very few up on deck these days.

Though it is impossible to count them, it is likely that over fifty have been tossed into an ocean grave during the past two weeks.

April 29. My condition has improved but Eileen has been confined to the cabin for two days. If anything should happen to her it would take all the meaning out of my life. I have been bribing the steward to give me a bit of nourishing food for her and she appears to be improving. Her medicine box is finally empty. She asked the mate a few days ago for a few remedies from the ship's supply but he told her that he wasn't running a hospital and that under no conditions would he permit her to dispense medicines.

May 4. We have been four weeks on the Naparima which is still bearing up and looks as if she will hold together for the rest of the journey.

This proved to be the most eventful day so far. Looking back on it I fail to see how I could have acted otherwise under the circumstances. I rose at daybreak. The ship was under full sail beating a northwest wind. My cousin Timmy had been doing some chores on deck. This morning the mate ordered him to go up the fore-mast to put to rights some tackle that got entangled in the last tack. There was a stiff wind and I think that at that height he was afraid. The mate yelled at him with his customary string of profanity. But Timmy was unable to get the mess untangled. The mate grabbed a rope's end and ordered him down. Cursing him for his awkwardness he seized his feet while they were still in the ratlines. The boy fell violently onto the deck. The mate proceeded to shower blows on the head and back of the prone victim with the heavy rope. That was as much as I could bear.

"Put down that rope, sir, and leave the boy alone. It is not his fault that he couldn't do a job that should be done by an experienced sailor." He glared at me with a look that meant murder.

"Mind your business, damn you, or I'll have you put in irons for mutiny."

He swung the rope again as I sprang at him and dealt him a blow in the face. He clutched me and we grappled. He was strong, with muscles toughened by years of fighting the wind and the sea. Nevertheless a Sligo boy of my build, even allowing for the weight I lost recently, will take odds from no man in a wrestling bout. In this case I had energy that I wouldn't normally possess, I was so incensed over the mate's conduct today as well as during our relationship in the past. We fell time and time again till I finally figured I had him down. But he managed to wriggle up again and I got a good hold of his neck. I got him down again and rained blows on every part of him that my right fist could reach. All of his cheating and cruelty flashed across my mind giving extra force to every blow. He was finally flattened out and I got up. By this time a crowd had gathered including most of the crew. Not one of them interfered. They stood off towards the forepeak and appeared pleased with the turn of events having all been victims of the mate's temper at one time or another.

The passengers had formed a circle around us during the fight. I noted that a few had Shillelaghs in their hands. After a few moments lying prone upon the deck my man got up and made as if to renew the fight. I gathered him up and, with strength born of fury, threw him across the deck. Fortunately for both of us he landed on a coil of rope. He lay there for a while until the steward came and helped him to his cabin. By this time excitement was running high among the passengers.

"If they try to lay a finger on you for what you have done we'll tear them to pieces," said one stout defender, waving a blackthorn in the air. I moved away as fast as I could. Softly opening the door of our cabin I was thankful to find Eileen still there mending clothing for some children. She was greatly alarmed over my appearance as I had taken quite a beating even though the mate fared worse. I explained briefly what had happened. Though relieved over the fact that I was not seriously injured she was concerned about the possible consequences of an attack on a ship's officer. But I am of the opinion that the fear of exposure will be my protection, provided we reach land before action is taken. I know too, however, that on board ship they can get away with anything. If the Captain takes matters into his own hands a summary settlement could take place any time. The boatswain told me this evening that the crew swore to a man to refuse to put a hand on me if the Captain orders my arrest. My cousin Timmy seems to have a stout bodyguard with him as he goes about his duties ever since the mate tried to beat him.

Though I do not feel any personal satisfaction over the results of the fight, the incident has brought a little much needed excitement into the painful monotony of trying, day after day, to endure the fearful hardships of life on board. Many of the passengers now have a feeling of at least a slight vindication of their rights as well as a sense of expectancy with regard to the possible outcome of the affair. They are determined to stand by me in case I run into more trouble. All I can do is to wait, taking care not to expose myself to any situation where the mate could suddenly attack me.

It took me two days to complete this entry. The mate must be licking his wounds. He has not appeared on deck since the fight.

May 7. There have been no more developments in the feud between the mate and myself. He is still in hiding. The Captain must know all about it by now. Knowing the mate as I do, I am sure that he will have his revenge.

We passed through large fields of ice yesterday. It takes great skill in handling the ship if a collision is to be avoided. We passed two ships caught in the ice. I am told that they will have to drift with it till the wind opens an escape channel.

A delightfully trim, two-masted vessel crossed our bow in the distance. She hoisted the Stars and Stripes. I feel sorry for the passengers who cannot come up and see the change in scenery as we move among ice fields. In stark contrast we also watch the ocean burials which are now a common sight.

Eileen and I spent part of the evening reviewing the journal. We both feel pleased over the picture it gives of Ireland today. It seems to recall, vividly in my own simple but truthful words, the state of ruin and sheer misery to which our country has been reduced. We hope and pray that her wounds are not mortal.

To see your bright face clouded so
 Like to the mournful moon. . .
The heart within my bosom faints,
To think of you my Queen,
My fond Rosaleen.

5

The St Lawrence

Crossing the Atlantic exacted a fearful toll. To say that about 20,000 perished on the ocean would be giving a very rough estimate. Who counted them, after all? To judge by the number of vessels and the average number of passengers and then using available lists of casualties we could truthfully say that there could have been 20,000 deaths on the ocean voyages, if we include the St Lawrence River.

"If crosses and tombs could be created on the water the whole route of the emigrant vessels from Ireland to America would have looked like a crowded cemetery," observed an emigration commissioner in the United States.

J. M.

May 9. The boatswain told us this morning that we may reach the Canadian quarantine station in two weeks. He added that navigating the St Lawrence River is a hazardous part of the voyage. It demands skill and watchfulness at all times.

Sundays on board have been no different from other

days of the week. A few times we planned to have a
worship service but the weather and the difficulty of
getting a space to gather made it impossible. Today the
weather was in our favour so we were able to get about a
hundred passengers together on deck. It was consoling to
pray together in the midst of our fears and troubles. With
conditions on board as they were there has been very
little time for devotional exercises of any kind. Eileen led
the group in two hymns. From her family Bible she
chose a Gospel reading. It was singularly appropriate. It
was the parable of the rich man and Lazarus. "There was
a certain rich man. . . and a beggar named Lazarus. . . .
But Abraham said, Son, remember that thou in thy
lifetime receivedst the good things and likewise Lazarus
evil things, but now he is comforted." This was followed
by a reading of the Beatitudes. Very frankly it is beyond
my powers of understanding to fathom what good there
can be in all the suffering and degradation that we are
witnessing during these tragic times. "Blessed are the
poor; blessed are they who suffer." I know that God can
reward the poor and the suffering, eventually, in
Paradise. But here and now these things are evil, the
product of the machinations of evil men. And we must
fight against them at every turn. The triumph of Lazarus
relates to another world, which we all hope to be a
Paradise, but here we are in a sort of hell. And sometimes
we are utterly helpless to improve our lot. Perhaps it is
only at this point that we should think of resignation and
hope for vindication in a future life.

May 12. Eileen and I spend some time every day
down below except when we ourselves are under the
weather. We rarely go down without seeing the work of
the grim reaper. A few times we had to look for one of
the volunteers to prepare a body for burial. They have
made up a kind of hammock for lifting the bodies up to

22. – Why do we exert ourselves so little to help one another, when it takes so little to please! Aileen coaxed the steward to let her have some discarded biscuit bags. These she is fashioning into a sort of gowns to cover the nakedness of several girls who could not come on deck. The first she finished this afternoon, and no aristocratic miss could have been prouder of her first silk dress than was the poor child of the transformed canvas bag, which was her only garment.

23. – This is Sunday. The only change in the routine of the ship that marks the day is that the sailors gave an extra wash down to the decks and after that did not work except trim the sails. They spent the forenoon on the forecastle mending or washing their clothes. During the afternoon it grew cold with a strong wind from the north-east, accompanied by driving showers. Towards sunset the sea was a lather of foam, and the wind had increased to a gale. When the waves began to flood the deck, the order was given to put the hatches on. God help the poor souls shut in beneath my feet!

From the original journal

the deck. It is often difficult to get enough cloth to wrap them in but the people are generous with their own bits of clothing even though they can ill afford to spare any. We were lashed all day yesterday by a strong north-west wind. It blew itself out during the night. Previous storms have soaked the Naparima's ancient timbers enough to partly seal the cracks where leaks were occurring. There is much less flooding in the hold now.

Recovery from the fever is hardly to be expected in the atmosphere of the dark dungeon to which the patients are confined, with no medical care and no nourishing food. But some are surviving and this is encouraging. We are doing all we can, including bribes to the steward, to bring soup and tea and scones to the most likely victims, the elderly, the weak and the children.

Once again we got a good number up on deck today. The sun is out and the ship is pitching and rolling gently on a glassy swell. The wind picked up this evening and the sails began flapping like gunshots. There is a heavy mist and though we are not yet six weeks out of Dublin there is talk of land not too far ahead. The boatswain claims that we are approaching a huge shoal called the Grand Banks, noted for its abundant supply of fish.

May 13. The mention of land has stirred up a wholesome wave of excitement and expectation among the passengers. Some of the men, experienced fishermen from the west coast of Sligo, are already getting organized to drop a line. They bargained with the cook for some line and hooks and a bit of salt pork for bait. When lead cast soundings indicated that we were on the Grand Banks they dropped their lines. After a long wait they finally struck a school of fish. Everybody who was able to walk was on deck to share the excitement of landing some choice cod and dogfish. By offering the cook a few of the best, the fishermen succeeded in getting him to cook a supply for the passengers. As is the custom among our people there was a joyful sharing of the catch. Some choice pieces were brought down to those who were unable to leave their bunks. Since the cook could not prepare enough for all on board the men have built a fire in the cooking area on deck and it looks as if the supply of food will continue for a while.

May 14. After our joyful celebration over the catch of fish we had to face another crisis. The drinking water, for a long time now, has been brackish and cloudy. We have tried to boil it whenever we could and cleared it by putting it through a strainer. But it is so filthy now that it is dangerous to use in any way.

My two little cousins, Ellen and Bridget O'Connor, have been sick for two days, unable to take any food. The steward has access to the ship's medicine supply and we were able to induce him, with a generous tip, to get us some tonic. It will, we hope, put the girls back on their feet. Fortunately Eileen's father left her all that remained of his savings, so we are in a position to get things like food and medicine that otherwise would be out of our reach. Uncle Jeremiah has been looking worse and worse since Aunt Mary died.

After about six weeks on the Atlantic we were treated to a very welcome sight this afternoon. A flock of birds flew over us. They were as welcome as the dove that flew back to Noah's ark with a twig in its mouth. To add to the excitement the sailors began to get the anchors off the forecastle and bitted to the catheads. It is a slow and laborious task. I haven't seen such movement and spirit among the passengers since we left Sligo.

May 16. Stepping out on deck this morning I was astonished to see land on either side. From a small chart that I have it looks like Cape North and St Paul Island.

The sunlight brought the lighthouses into sharp relief. I hurried down below to announce the news. In no time there was a large, excited crowd on deck. To my delight I even saw two children playing near the hatchway. They too are picking up the good news. Their survival in the hold for the past six weeks is some kind of miracle. Good news is contagious. Ellen and Bridget are up and around and Timmy was able to speak to them for a few moments. The mate is still keeping out of sight, otherwise things like this could not happen.

May 18. A fantastic group of lonely islets of rocks worn into dramatic forms shooting straight up from the sea, came into view today. While watching these rugged sentinels of the mighty gulf of the St Lawrence River that we were entering, my eye chanced to fall on the face of an elderly woman Eileen was ministering to on deck. She apparently collapsed as soon as she came up from the hold. I recognized her as Mrs Finnegan of the tea episode. More pinched and sallow her complexion could not be. She was wasted and worn to a skeleton. How she ever managed to get up is a mystery. The lines of her face bespoke great suffering. I got her a tin of water that had been boiled. She motioned it away with a wan smile. Her soul was plainly quitting her frail body but it delayed momentarily for the pathetic caresses of a young girl, her grandchild, who had become an orphan on the way over. Mrs Finnegan did not die of the fever. She succumbed to the onslaught of all the other distresses that the poor emigrants are confronted with in this criminal traffic in human beings. We buried her with as much dignity as we could bring to the ceremony and became the custodians of another orphan girl.

May 19. I had been in bed for some time last night when I was disturbed by voices outside. I dressed and went out. The boatswain was pointing to the sky and talking excitedly to some of the crew. The sails, rope and block were motionless. Thousands of eerie-looking clouds, all spherical in shape and set in a pattern of mathematical regularity, made a ghostly picture overhead. It looked as if the ship was standing under the dome of a weird world. The scene was reflected in wavy patterns on the surface of the water. In answer to a remark I made about it the boatswain said: "It ain't weather, sir, it's death. We're in for something bad. All you have to do is read the signs up above." I stayed out for a long time watching the show.

After surviving the dangerous moods of the Atlantic, ships bound for Canadian ports still have the hazards of the St Lawrence River to face. Local pilots are the only ones who know how to steer clear of danger. But owing to the heavy traffic in emigrants there are not enough seasoned pilots for all the ships. The Mingan Rocks, for example – they were pointed out to me by a crew member – have been the scene of several tragedies. One of the emigrant ships, I am told, was wrecked on the rocks early in May and there was not a single survivor.

Without an experienced river pilot the regular Captain has to try to navigate the river. The man at the wheel has to be always on the alert for a sudden change in course ordered by the Captain who has extra lookouts on duty. All this means that there are times of dreadful suspense when low rocky islands appear suddenly and a ship has to turn on her heel with every able body on deck hauling on the ropes. Shipwreck for some, they say, has meant landing on an uninhabited, barren island, faced with death from starvation and exposure.

May 20. We were fortunate enough to be boarded by a river pilot who immediately took command of the ship and never leaves the poop. He is a Frenchman, sturdy and bronzed and smiling and he seems to be in full command of the situation. This afternoon we saw mast tops above the fog and soon sighted a large stately vessel, clean-looking and in splendid order. Coming close, our Captain asked if he had a pilot. He said that he had none. Our Captain invited him to follow but in a few minutes he was out of sight ahead of us. The ship was from either Holland or Germany.

Later on this evening a thunderous sound of rattling told us that the order had been given to drop anchor. Our pilot considered the fog too dense to challenge in this area.

May 21. The scenery today is magnificent. Our ship is the only thing out of harmony with Nature's splendour. There has been a frightening increase in the number of fever cases this week. We are becoming a floating charnel house on what must be one of the world's grandest rivers. There are two or three burials a day since last week. It is sad to see so many struck down almost in sight of our destination. Those who come up on deck during the day look more and more like spectres. The six weeks on hardtack and tea has weakened many of them while the general atmosphere of the hold has brought them down both emotionally and physically.

May 22. Our progress up-river is very slow. It is far from being a monotonous part of the voyage, for those who are well enough to enjoy it, for the scenery continues to be dazzling. I have said that we Irish consider our own country to be very beautiful, but if Canada is at all like what we see here along the St Lawrence River we are just moving from one of the world's choicest lands to another. A charming landscape is continually unfolding before us. The north shore along here is rugged, with lofty wooded hills, while the south shore is an undulating slope dotted with small white-coloured farmhouses. Farms run like rubands from the river to the upper part of the slope. At regular intervals there are churches built of stone, with high-pitched roofs and tin-covered steeples, giving a foreign look to the edifices. Towards the other side of the river there are four ships waiting like ourselves for the tide to turn. At least two of them appear to be emigrant ships.

Towards midday two men approached us from the shore in a small boat. They had provisions to sell but did not fancy the appearance of our boat and its passengers for they did not throw us a line. One of them said to the mate who is now making appearances on deck: "Parlez-vous français?" "Blast your impudence" said the mate, "Who do you think my mother was? I want none of your lingo." Seemingly disgusted with the whole situation they were about to pull away when I mustered a bit of French that I know and addressed them. "Avez-vous du lait ou du pain?" I asked them. One of the men caught a pail I lowered and filled it with milk while the other tied three loaves of bread to the rope holding the pail. He held up five fingers for the price. I figured he meant five shillings which I lowered to him with the rope. They seemed satisfied but they couldn't have been as pleased as we were to be able to give out milk and bread to the children and to the sick.

This evening, with a large spread of canvas, we moved up the river.

May 23. The landscape continues to be a feast for the eyes. The clear, deep, blue water of the St Lawrence reflects islands while the bold, stately forests stand out in marked contrast with the gently rolling landscapes to the southeast. A few billowy clouds floating in the tender blue sky complete the picture. We succeeded in getting most of the passengers on deck to enjoy the show. Scenes like this should help cancel out the memory of the dark, sorrowful days and nights that we have gone through.

Eileen and I were leaning over the bulwark this afternoon when we spied a dark looking object floating by us. It was the hideously wasted body of a victim from one of the vessels ahead of us. The body didn't even have any kind of a burial shroud.

Deck hand Martin Riley told us today about one ship that lost all on board back at the Mingan Rocks which I referred to a few days ago. The ship crashed on the rocks and over three hundred perished. The boatswain confirmed Riley's account of the wreck and added that several ships had become wrecked along the shores where the loss of life was considerable.

It was surprising to me to learn that we were far from being the first to depart from Ireland. Dozens of vessels left, principally from Cork and Dublin and Liverpool towards the end of March and the beginning of April. It is reported that they were all overloaded, like the Naparima, with Ireland's leading export, human beings.

May 24. The mate is still giving me a wide berth. The people are aware of the danger I am in and some of the men are keeping a close watch over me. There will be a squaring of accounts, I am sure, before our final parting. He has the law on his side for it is a serious offence to assault a ship's officer. He will likely settle the score personally if he can.

While beating up the river, a Clyde trader overhauled us today. Being shorter she wore more quickly and, with her heavy load, she was able to sail closer to the wind. As she passed, her Captain dangled a rope at the stern as if offering to take our ship in tow. But our Captain was in no mood for joking. He turned down the companionway with an oath and disappeared.

Another joyful incident took place this afternoon. A

As we made our way up the glorious river, the shores trended nearer, the hills on the north grew loftier and the southern bank less steep. The sun had set in a glory of gold and crimson beyond the hills when the order was given to let go the anchor, the tide no longer serving us. Quarter a mile ahead of us a large ship did the same. The evening being calm Aileen got a wrap and we sat watching the darkening waters and the shores that loomed momentarily more faint, until the lights from the house windows alone marked where they were. "What is that?" she suddenly exclaimed, and I saw a shapeless heap move past our ship on the outgoing tide. Presently there was another and another. Craning my head over the bulwark I watched. Another came, it caught in our cable, and before the swish of the current washed it clear, I caught a glimpse of a white face. I understood it all. The ship ahead of us had emigrants and they were throwing overboard their dead. Without telling Aileen, I grasped her arm, and drew her to our cabin.

From the original journal

boy hauled up a pail of water to wash. He tasted the water, it looked so good, and found out that it was fresh. Pailful after pailful was hauled up. Everybody was supplied unstintingly with clear, sweet, cool water. The ship's supply is nothing short of sewage. It has surely contributed to the wave of sickness among the passengers. In spite of their being warned about the danger of drinking it without making sure it is boiled, some slaked their burning thirst with what they got direct from the supply.

The shocking sight of bodies floating in the river is becoming common now. As for ourselves, though we are free from the violence of the ocean storms and well supplied with fresh water and fish, there is no let-up in the progress of the fever.

Yesterday we had five deaths. I asked the boatswain if, from now on, we might keep the bodies for burial on land since we were so near to our destination. He said that it might take three or four more days on account of the slow progress of the river. We are concerned now about taking water from the river which is serving as a graveyard for the fleet of floating pesthouses that is contaminating it.

We remained at anchor all day today. Strong north-west winds defiantly held the Naparima motionless. A fair wind would see us at our destination in about a day, yet we cannot advance a yard. There were five more deaths today. In spite of all our efforts the condition of the hold remains filthy. All our efforts to control the fever seem to be futile.

All hands among the crew are frantically engaged at the task of putting the vessel into her best trim. They are scrubbing, painting and scraping every bit of the deck. They have strict orders to put on a good show for the inspecting officers at the quarantine station so that the Naparima may go ahead with her nefarious trade. The appearance of her decks now belies the putrid condition of the passengers' quarters down below but I am sure that no inspector will go down there. As a final touch they are having the steps leading to the dungeon scrubbed. The steward bribed a few passengers with a shot of whiskey to do the job.

May 25. The wind has changed so we may land any time now. We have been over seven weeks confined to this floating tub of a vessel. But perhaps we should be thankful since some emigrant boats take up to eleven or twelve weeks to reach the end of the journey.

As I write this note I hear the sound of anchor being weighed. It was music to my ears. Eileen, who has been feeling very fatigued for the past few days, is all smiles. I am too excited to write any more this evening.

May 26. We went out on deck early this morning. From a little country church along the shore came the pealing of a bell announcing an early Mass. The most amazing sight of all is the number of ships ahead of us, behind us, all around us, most of them at anchor. Like the Naparima they too are in ship shape for inspection. We have no doubt about the dark, pestilential dungeons that lie hid below their decks.

We are moving slowly past a group of islands. I am told that the last one of the group is Grosse Ile, where we are due to be inspected. Those who do not have the fever will go on to Quebec.

I am making this entry in the early afternoon as we may be at quarantine this evening. Eileen is packing our few belongings in case we change boats. The passengers too are getting ready. Four more died this morning. The bodies will be held for burial on land. For about a hundred down below there is no taste of excitement or of anticipation for they are lying in their bunks, unable to move.

Timmy came rushing to our cabin with the news that we are in sight of Grosse Ile. This may be my last note on board.

May 27. They were in no hurry getting us on board when we left Ireland and now they appear to be in no hurry getting us landed. Last night the Naparima, about eight weeks out from Dublin, weighed anchor off Grosse Ile. She hoisted her ensign as a signal for the inspecting officers. Unless there is a large staff of inspectors we could have a long wait. There are thirty or forty other vessels anchored in the river. After waiting all day today a medical officer finally boarded the Naparima. All the passengers who were able to stand up were marched by him. Those who showed signs of infection were herded into a group. They, together with the ones down below, are to be landed at the quarantine hospital. The inspector rushed through his job, had a visit with the captain and left hurriedly. While waiting for further developments I took time to write this note in my journal.

Whether or not I will write any more I do not know at this time. I have told, in my own simple way, the story of how the poor and the dispossessed and the patriots are being treated in my country. I have tried to give a word picture of the intensity of their sufferings and, above all, of the indignities which have been heaped upon them. My only regret is the limitations that words have, in any attempt to use them to express the unfathomable depths of misery to which countless thousands have been reduced by famine and pestilence and persecution. If our trials stemmed from natural causes, from all those contingencies and disasters that are legally classified as acts of God, they would in many ways be more bearable. But the famine was an artificial one and pestilence followed naturally in its wake. After being deprived of food and the basic right to possess land freely in our own country, we were subjected to ruthless persecution by hordes of ruffians who were hired to molest us in every possible way. The final blow for all of the dispossessed was to be driven from our land and transported, in the holds of the most dilapidated vessels in the world, to a foreign land. Far from exaggerating anything in this story, I have merely touched the surface of the massive tragedy. If this is the end of my story I sincerely hope that it contains enough of the truth to let the world know how sorely we have been tried by the tribulations we have endured.

May 28. For some unknown reason we had to remain overnight on the Naparima. It may be that orders came from on shore to delay landing of the sick for there is a swarm of landing boats already at the dock. I found out last night that ships are sometimes delayed several days waiting on inspection and orders to land the sick. I got my journal out of the box once again as I have several things to relate on this day's events.

We are all amazed at the general appearance of the quarantine station. First of all the landing dock is in disgraceful condition. With its broken planks and unsteady supports it makes the landing of the sick a difficult and dangerous operation. What is more surprising is the two large sheds with bunks not far from the landing area. Surely this is not the Canadian quarantine hospital! There is a substantial structure to the east of the sheds but it could hardly be expected to accommodate even a small fraction of the crowds that are being landed. We cannot get a good view of the sheds from our ship but it looks as if the bunks are already occupied. All in all it is a very primitive looking quarantine station.

We had a delightful little interlude today in the monotony of the delay. Two clergymen, a Roman Catholic priest and an Anglican, paid us a visit. They had no hesitation about descending to the hold to minister to the sick and dying. The warm reception they got proves that our people have kept the Faith even when all their earthly hopes were dashed. Before leaving, the clergymen stopped for a chat with the crowd on deck.

Eileen just came to tell me that they are lowering the boats to bring the sick ashore. While it is heartrending to see so many of our people destined for whatever ordeals face the fever victims on the island, we are relieved to know that our own ordeal is coming to an end. We hope to be in Quebec by tonight. So ends our honeymoon.

6

Grosse Ile

There came to the beach a poor exile of Erin.

Once again I lay my journal aside hoping to add a conclusion when we arrive at Quebec. They are calling now for volunteers to bring the sick and the dead to shore. The sailors are refusing to have anything to do with the task. Timmy tells me that the mate offered to pay them for the work. A few have accepted the offer. I feel it my duty to render what will be my last service to these poor suffering creatures in offering myself as a volunteer. Eileen is helping to get them ready for the boats.

June 2. After four days and five nights of confusion and mental anguish, I sorrowfully take up my journal again. The mate finally got even with me. Fiendishly and cunningly he planned my destruction. I will relate briefly how it all happened.

Transporting the sick to shore turned out to be a heartrending task. With indecent haste we had to rush them from the deck into the boats and then leave them lying on the dock. There was no provision for having them carried to whatever quarters they were to be housed in. On account of the neglected condition of the landing place their pain-racked bodies received further shocks. We moved seven dead bodies in one boat. I met a young French priest who was most compassionate and considerate in lending a hand. We loaded the bodies onto a little wagon where the priest pronounced a blessing over them and went to attend to the sick.

Back on the dock I got the shock of a lifetime. There was Eileen standing among the sick, waiting on me.

"Why do you look at me so? I have come as you requested," she said.

When I told her angrily that I never sent for her she replied that the steward gave her a message telling her that I wanted her on shore with the luggage. Looking out on the river I saw that the Naparima had tripped anchor and was headed towards Quebec. Since Eileen and I passed the medical inspection we were supposed to be landed at Quebec. The mate won the last round of the fight. He could not have punished me more severely with the end of a rope. I went to the head doctor, Doctor Douglas, and explained the matter to him. He told me that there would be a steamer leaving the island in a week. It would drop us at Quebec.

June 3. How I cursed myself for my rashness in making the Captain and the mate my enemies. Seeing Eileen exposed to the frightful conditions on this island causes me intense anxiety. The revenge has fallen on her.

Not wishing to be near the fever sheds I sought for a place of shelter. The only thing in sight was an abandoned little lean-to which we occupied for the moment. It had a bit of straw which we covered with a blanket to provide a place to sleep at night. I went to the cooking booth near the sheds and got a loaf of bread and some tea for two shillings. Eileen couldn't eat though she tried, just to please me. I fear for the worst. She may be getting the fever. Though the weather is mild it has started to rain and a fresh east wind penetrates the shelter. Making her as comfortable as I could, on the bed of straw, I prayed as I never have before. I am adding this little item to my journal with our little box on my knees and a candle stuck to the corner of it. Unable to sleep, I find that this passes the time.

June 4. When morning came today Eileen was unable to move. Fever and chill alternated. I looked in vain for a doctor. Beyond giving her a bit of water I was helpless. Towards evening a doctor, yielding to my importunities, came to see her. He gave me a note and told me to take it to the hospital steward. I fairly ran back with the medicine.

June 8. After the last few dreadful days and nights I went through I never thought I'd have the heart to pick up the journal again. I am alone now and feel I have nothing to live for. Eileen is dead. I only wish I were with her.

For three days I watched her as she went through spasms of racking pain and raging fever, in and out of periods of delirium. This afternoon with bursting heart and throbbing head I knelt by as the life ebbed out of her. I clasped her in my arms as the whole nightmarish past flew through my mind. I closed her eyes, laid her down ever so tenderly and went to look for help. I saw a priest coming out of the little church and approached him. His name was Father McGoran, an Irishman. "If I had only known," he said "I could have offered you a decent place to stay." He came to the shelter where he said some prayers for the repose of my dear departed. He reminded me that, hard as it may be, she would have to be buried without delay. He explained that the burial place was a field at the west end of the island where the dead were tossed five and six deep in trenches. We agreed that somehow Eileen's remains should be spared this final indignity. I asked for a shovel, intending to dig a grave in a secret spot, mindful of the fact that the authorities would not approve. Father McGoran got one from behind the church and helped me to carry the body to a wooded knoll towards the north side of the island. We found a place completely hidden by trees. There we reverently buried the most beautiful girl in all the world.

I was invited to take a cot in a little cabin sometimes used by the clergy. Here tonight I feel that I am the loneliest man in the world, driven by the need to express my sorrows, so I have added these lines. Nothing in the world could induce me to leave this island now. Its earth encloses all that I hold dear in this world.

June 9. This morning Father McGoran brought me a bite to eat and promised to come back around noon hour. After my tea I immediately set out to visit the grave. I carried a small cross I made last night, with the name Eileen on it. Propped up against a tree I sat by the grave all morning. Overwhelmed by grief and unnerved from loss of sleep, my mind was somewhere between reality and a world of fantasy. Could all these little tragedies, compressed into a few months, have been just a bad dream? But there was the grave and it was real. In a daze I walked back to the little cabin where Father McGoran was waiting for me. I am thankful that he did not try to get me to smother my grief. He did, however, ask me to help out here and there since there were hundreds of sick getting no attention as a result of the shortage of doctors, nurses and attendants in general.

June 10. Last night I had snatches of sleep with horrible

Leaving the cemetery with the priest, I thanked him from my heart, and ran to the quay. My heart was in my mouth when I saw on it Aileen, standing beside our boxes, and the ship, having tripped her anchor, bearing up the river. "What makes you look so at me, Gerald? I have come as you asked."

"I never sent for you."

"The steward told me you had sent word by the sailors for me to come ashore, that you were going to stay here. They carried the luggage into a boat and I followed."

I groaned in spirit. I saw it all. By a villainous trick, the captain had got rid of me. Instead of being in Quebec that day, here I was left at the quarantine station. "My poor Aileen, I know not what to do; my trouble is for you." I went to see the head of the establishment, Dr Douglas. He proved to be a fussy gentleman, worried over a number of details. Professing to be ready to oblige, he said there was no help for me until the steamer came. "When will that be?" Next Saturday. A week on an island full of people sick with fever! Aileen, brave heart, made the best of it. She was soaking wet, yet the only shelter, apart

From the original journal

from the fever sheds, which were not to be thought of, was an outhouse with a leaky roof, with no possibility of a fire or change of clothing. How I cursed myself for my rashness in making captain and mate my enemies, for the penalty had fallen not on me, but on my Aileen. There was not an armful of straw to be had; not even boards to lie on. I went to the cooking booth, and found a Frenchman in charge. Bribing him with a shilling he gave me a loaf and a tin of hot tea. Aileen could not eat a bite, though she tried to do to please me, but drank the tea. The rain continued and the east wind penetrated between the boards of the wretched sheiling. What a night it was! I put my coat over Aileen, I pressed her to my bosom to impart some heat to her chilled frame, I endeavoured to cheer her with prospects of the morrow. Alas, when morning came she was unable to move, and fever and chill alternated. I sought the doctor, he was not to be had. Other emigrant ships had arrived, and he was visiting them. Beyond giving her water to assuage her thirst when in the fever it was not in my power to do anything. It was evening when the doctor, yielding to my importunities, came to see her. He did not stay a

From the original journal

minute and writing a few lines told me to go to the hospital steward, who would give me some medicine. Why recall the dreadful nights and days that followed? What profit to tell of the pain in the breast, the raging fever, the delirium, the agonizing gasping for breath — the end? The fourth day, with bursting heart and throbbing head, I knelt by the corpse of my Aileen. There was not a soul to help; everybody was too full of their own troubles to be able to heed me. The island was now filled with sick emigrants, and death was on every side. I dug her grave, the priest came, I laid her there, I filled it in, I staggered to the shed that had sheltered us, I fell from sheer exhaustion, and remember no more. When I woke, I heard the patter of rain, and felt so inexpressibly weary I could think of nothing, much less make any exertion. My eye fell on Aileen's shawl, and the past rushed on me. Oh, the agony of that hour; my remorse, my sorrow, my beseechings of the Unseen. Such a paroxysm could not last long, and when exhausted nature compelled me to lie down, I turned my face to the wall with the earnest prayer I might never awaken on this earth.

From the original journal

dreams of being suffocated by mysterious powers. I became fully awake before dawn. A feeling of inexpressible weariness and even of indifference to life makes me wonder if I would be of any use as a helper, in the way Father McGoran suggested. Turning my face to the wall where I could barely discern the outline of Eileen's shawl, I only wished that I could fall asleep never to wake up. But I must not, I realize, let my grief become a luxury. Thousands of my dear people have gone through trials just as severe as mine. I must have dozed off around sunrise only to be awakened by someone leaning over me with the greeting "Pax tecum." It was none other than Father Tom O'Hare. The Bishop counselled him to join the emigrants so as to avoid being arrested for his outspoken remarks and daring actions back home. He sailed on the Urania, from Cork. After hearing my sad story he expressed his deep and genuine sorrow. He had gone on to Quebec where he met my cousin Timmy. On being told Eileen and I were on the island he volunteered for service here. Meeting with him has been balm for my wounds.

I spent a few hours at Eileen's grave today. Tomorrow I am to start helping out as an attendant among the sick. The fever sheds are a fearful sight. All day long I can hear the sound of moaning and the cries of the fever patients for water. But there is nothing that I fear now. I am ready to offer myself in any way as a kind of reparation for my part in the events that led to Eileen's untimely death.

June 11. I am determined to keep my journal up to date right to the end whatever that may be. I am sure that the outside world knows nothing about this final act of our tragedy, the holocaust on this lonely island.

Father McGoran introduced me to Doctor Douglas, the chief medical officer here. He is the doctor who gave me the medicine for Eileen. He welcomed me and put me in charge of rendering whatever services I could in one of the sheds which was just being filled with patients from a ship. I already had a lot of experience in the hold of the Naparima with Eileen as my teacher. I went to work with zest, helping to settle the patients in their bunks, getting them fresh water and what food I could muster, and calling for the services of a doctor or clergyman for the critically ill. There is some sort of healing of our emotional and spiritual scars in the very act of performing the corporal works of mercy and though I have been ministering for only one day my grief is already becoming more rational. My blind sorrow is being directed into practical compassion for the hundreds of suffering victims in the fever sheds. Whether or not it comes from an overwrought imagination I cannot say but in some mysterious way Eileen is present with me as I make my rounds. This does not prevent me from keeping my two-hour daily watch at the lonely grave hidden among the bushes up on the hill.

June 12. I have to learn to acquire a reasonable amount of detachment in my contacts with the suffering and dying. Most of them are in such a deplorable condition from illness, hunger and neglect that, if I let myself go, I would fall apart from the very sight of their intense misery. It is, however, very difficult to be detached when in so many ways they try to express their gratitude for my simple services. I spent most of the day today with tears in my eyes.

At noon hour I had tea and a few biscuits with Father McGoran and two young French priests from Quebec. These men, together with the doctors, are the heroes in this mass tragedy. They appear to be on the go day and night with no concern for their own safety. They spoke of trying to urge the Canadian government to erect more

sheds and send more medical help. They are also trying
to get food for the starving.

There is an endless line of ships out in the harbour
today. The quarantine station is already woefully
understaffed and overcrowded with patients and I
wonder what will become of all the sick and dying out
on those ships. Today they began to put up tents to take
some of the overflow. It is incredible that the Canadian
government is not taking emergency measures. But as I
see it there is no Canadian government as such. Canada is
ruled by the Home Office and we can expect no better
treatment here than what we had in Ireland.

June 13. Today is Sunday. It was neither a day of rest
nor of religious observance though I had the privilege of
attending a Mass in the little church, offered by Father
O'Hare, for the repose of the soul of my dear departed
one. Like all the others I set out immediately after Mass
on my daily rounds. Here is my destiny. What better way
to spend my days than in serving people who are going
through some of the agony that I felt, the agony of
separation from family and friends through death and as a
result of the way people were dispersed on leaving the
ships. Most of the people I have met so far in the fever
sheds have tearfully asked me if I could locate a dear one.
I have written down as many names as I can remember
each day though there is little hope that anything can be
done.

In all the confusion and darkness of the past week or
so I forgot to look for Uncle Jeremiah and the two girls,
Ellen and Bridget. I knew they were put off here. To my
delight I discovered them today. The two girls were
recovering but Uncle Jeremiah was in very poor
condition. The news about Eileen was a shock to them
for they loved her very much. Like most of the bunks in
the sheds theirs was filthy. Too sick to do anything for

themselves and unable to get the ear of an attendant they had let things go. I set about cleaning up and putting things in order. What clothing they could do without for the moment I took to the river to wash. Fortunately they received food regularly – soup and biscuits.

Among all the mournful sounds coming from the suffering masses in the sheds there is one that haunts me, even when I am out of ear shot, and that is the plaintive pleas of the fever victims for water. It is, apparently, of questionable value as a restorative for a patient with a high fever but, from what I have observed so far, it is often the last service offered to the dying before death releases them. I have also observed that, in their utter loneliness and complete separation from family and friends, they are immeasurably uplifted and consoled by a little act of compassion whether it be the simple act of holding a noggin of water to their lips or helping to make them more comfortable in the bunk. Another thing I learned – it was suggested by Father McGoran – is to say a little prayer for them. I am somewhat out of character in doing this as I am not at all demonstrative in the exercise of my religion. But it works like magic in getting a response from them. My favourite is the expression Father O'Hare greeted me with, *Pax tecum* – Peace be to you.

The quarantine island is a little world of disquieting sounds. Besides the sad symphony of cries of pain and mental anguish in the fever sheds we can hear, day and night, a sinister reminder of the daily harvest collection of the grim reaper. It is the sound of the little wagons as they haul the dead to the west end of the island where the burial trenches are located. This goes on day and night. They take up to ten bodies each trip. It has been estimated that on a bad day the casualties can be a hundred or more. Yesterday we counted thirty-seven vessels out in the harbour. Some drop as many as two or three hundred at quarantine. And this is only a fraction of the ghost fleet. At the present rate many thousands of the victims will end up in the burial trenches. Many have escaped from the fever sheds only to drop dead among the bushes in remote areas of the island.

June 14. When I was on my way this evening to visit Eileen's grave, Father McGoran intercepted me and invited me to take a walk around the island. It appears to be about a mile wide and perhaps two miles in length. In my mind it is a Nature Paradise. And man has made a temporary hell out of it.

There is an abundance of song birds, rabbits, squirrels and chipmunks. Some of the animals must have crossed at a time when the river froze or else they were brought over in captivity and released. The island is noted as a game reserve for it is on the main migration routes of the geese. On the north side there is a chain of wooded hills. We walked by the burial trenches. A load of bodies arrived and the carriers literally shovelled them into the trenches and threw a bit of earth over them. I had to move away quickly for it was a sorry spectacle. The hospital at the other end of the island is a well-built structure though it is practically useless in a mass disaster such as we now have at the quarantine. The fever sheds stand out as an ugly scar on the open area of the landscape.

While we walked, my companion told me about a visit to a ship yesterday. He was called to administer the last rites to the dying. He said that he would never, till his dying day, forget the sight of the hold of that ship. Slightly more than five feet high, it had every side lined with berths containing the dead and dying. The filth of the place and the foul air made him wonder how any one could stay alive there even for a matter of hours. I couldn't help but add that this was a good description of the Naparima.

June 15. My nights are infinitely lonely without Eileen. Her shawl, the only souvenir I have of her, hangs on the wall near my cot. During the day my work takes my mind off the overwhelming feeling of loneliness that grips me during the night. Yet I would rather drink my cup of sorrow to the dregs than have my grief dissolved. There is no sickness that can match loneliness in the blow it deals to both body and soul. Eileen was a saintly person in her natural goodness and my sole consolation is that, as sure as there is a life beyond this one, she is now in a state of bliss.

I am able to put in up to eighteen hours a day in the performance of my humble services. There are still hundreds of patients who are just lying in their berths without receiving any attention. The crowding and the filth are almost as bad as on the ships. The berths are in tiers so that the people in the lower ones are targets for whatever waste and even excreta fall from above. The sheds were built to accommodate about two hundred patients. Flimsy extensions had to be added when instead of hundreds, thousands began to arrive. People are huddled together with no regard for age or sex and left to die or to survive on their own resources. At long intervals attendants arrive with food and water. The dead are removed only at certain fixed hours with the result that the living often have to lie for hours beside a corpse. Needless to say, with the crowding and confusion, two patients are commonly crowded into one narrow berth. The few doctors on the island can see only a very small fraction of the critically ill. They, together with the clergy, are a different breed of human beings from the selfish, unprincipled individuals who are the cause of this massive holocaust. They are dedicating themselves, without counting the cost, to the service of the sick.

The government has had several warnings about the hopeless inadequacy of the facilities here. Even now, in this state of emergency, practically nothing is being done. As an example of how desperate the situation is, they had to open the jails in Quebec to bolster the staff of helpers. The extra help they got are mostly hirelings who have no real interest in the problems of the patients. A lot of them are moral derelicts given to heavy drinking and carousing late at night. An army unit has been posted on the island to keep order but, from what I hear, the soldiers are at the root of most of the disorder among the attendants.

I had a word this evening with an outstanding member of the clergy here. His name is George Jehosephat Mountain. He is the leader of the Anglican clergy on the island. Though only about one in ten among the patients is Anglican, Reverend Mountain and his zealous assistants are on the move day and night, helping in every possible way. They go out of their way to get a priest for a Catholic patient who asks for one. There are about fifteen Catholic priests trying to keep up with the un-limited requests for assistance, whether it be for spiritual ministerings or for help in one of the many kinds of distress the suffering masses have to face in their struggle to survive. If it were not for this courageous band of volunteers the lot of the suffering and dying would be infinitely worse. Their very presence, as they move along the rows of berths in the sheds, is a powerful symbol of hope and comfort.

Reverend Mountain told me that he never experienced anything that could match the spiritual strength of the patients he met. He said he never heard an expression of bitterness or a querulous word from any of them. Even when the life was almost snuffed out of them from the ravages of fever and its accompanying chain of revolting symptoms, they invariably managed a word or an expression of thanks for services rendered. I heartily agree with what he said. He added that, in his opinion, it was not mere passive resignation or

"What interest can the Canadian government have in acting so?"

"No interest. It is more heedlessness than intent. The politicians are too absorbed in their paltry strifes to give heed to a few thousand Irish emigrants dying at their door."

"It sounds incredible."

"That is because you do not know politics and politicians here. I tell you, Gerald, I have been in Canada now three years, and (always barring the tools of the Irish landlords) if there be a more despicable creature than the office-hunting Canadian politician, I have yet to see him."

"If I must act, I should go first to Quebec to see after my people. They were promised ten shillings a head, to be paid by Lord Palmerston's agent at Quebec, and a deed from the Canadian government for a hundred acres a family."

"Faugh! Not a shilling, not an acre did they get. I saw them. Lord Palmerston has no agent in Quebec, the government will give no free grant of land. Mere lies told the poor crathurs to get them to leave Ireland."

From the original journal

indifference to their fate that prompted them to exhibit such inner strength. In his words, "It is the triumph of the spirit over forces that are bent on destroying them completely."

This little journal of mine, together with my daily round of duties, is helping to rescue me from the despair I felt when I lost Eileen. Doctor Douglas and Father McGoran advised me to leave this place, for my own good, though they seem to appreciate what I am doing. I am determined to stay, if possible to the end of my days. Everybody who comes here knows that the whole place is reeking with pestilence. The risk of becoming infected is great. I will not deliberately expose myself to any danger, beyond what I am necessarily exposed to, in the performance of the duties assigned to me. But if I should end my life as a result of my close contact with the fever victims, death would come as a liberator rather than a destroyer. If I have to face the future I know that I can do it but, as a result of the loss I have suffered, the prospect of death on this field of battle is not at all frightening.

June 17. There is one vessel that has been out in the harbour for a week with all the passengers still on board and with no assistance in the matter of food and medical supplies. Two priests went out to visit the ship and they reported about two hundred sick on board. The passengers said that the trip, which took nine weeks, was a nightmare. There were eleven dead in the hold and the crew has been paid to slip them into the river at nighttime. Doctor Douglas was notified. He said that he could not send out any assistance without orders from a government official. He finally took matters into his own hands and despatched food and medicine. Some sailors were put to work this afternoon with spars and sails to erect shelters for the sick. The sheds are all overcrowded.

Doctor Douglas told us that he sent a delegation to the government, in Montreal, about a week ago. After waiting outside his office for over two hours they finally got to see Mr Draper. He was civil but somewhat aloof. He said that his government had more pressing matters to attend to at the moment and that they should go to the provincial secretary. The provincial secretary was nowhere to be found. They went back to Draper's office. He warned them they must not heed alarmists who, he said, were giving too much publicity to the Grosse Ile affair. He dismissed them with the observation that the government was doing everything in its power to alleviate the situation. On hearing this the members of the delegation realized that any appeal to the government would be a waste of time.

June 18. Uncle Jeremiah is rallying physically but his mind has been affected by the heavy bout of fever he went through as well as by the trials that he has borne during the past few months.

On being told that another shipload of emigrants from Sligo was in the harbour I went out with Father O'Hare to see how the passengers fared. Dead bodies were being loaded by the dozen into boats manned by the sailors who were paid one sovereign for each body they brought to shore. Conditions on the boat were even worse than on the Naparima. In this case however, the Captain was not to blame. He was a good Christian gentleman who did everything in his power to help the passengers. His load of emigrants were from the northeast section of Lord Palmerston's estate where they lived in extreme poverty and where famine and fever claimed many victims. The Captain was helping with the removal of the bodies when we arrived.

This afternoon they were bringing in the sick from as far as two miles out in the river where the latest ships to

arrive are anchored. The number of patients on the island
has doubled in the past two weeks but there has been no
increase in the quantity of supplies coming in from
Quebec. Apparently it would take a special order from
the government to have the quantity increased.

A steamship, the first one I've ever seen, stopped in
the harbour today to pick up passengers for Montreal.
Though the Naparima was overloaded it couldn't compare
with the way the steamship was packed with passengers.
From shore where we had a good view it looked as if
about a thousand were crowded onto the decks. Father
McGoran told me that the trip to Montreal was even
worse than the ocean crossing. The people are two days
without shelter and without any food except what they
can bring with them. Many reach Montreal more dead
than alive. If we had only known about some of these
things back home when we elected for emigration, we
would certainly have chosen to face the odds there rather
than embark on this nightmare.

On the way to my watch at Eileen's grave today I
found the body of a man in a thicket nearby. He had
crawled there, away from the horrible sights and sounds
of the fever sheds, to die in peace. Though the hours I
spend beside the remains of my dear one bring me face to
face with the stark reality of my bereavement, they are
hours of deep meditation on the whole meaning of life in
the midst of a holocaust. What meaning can I attach to
the destruction of the beautiful young girl buried on this
God-forsaken island? My Faith tells me that all such
seeming contradictions will be rectified and all injustices
vindicated in another world. This belief brings me little,
if any, consolation as I face the loss of one who was an
intimate part of my very self. While it would be utterly
repulsive, even irrational, for me to think for a moment
that Eileen does not continue to exist beyond the grim
reality of death, yet the separation and the severe loss and

the outward destruction that death brings about, leave us with nothing but a sense of complete desolation.

I am spending part of my almost sleepless nights adding to this little account of what looks like the final act in the mass tragedy of this summer of sorrow.

June 19. I fear that they will have to send another military unit to control the company of guards who are already here. Their conduct is becoming increasingly unruly. The island would be much better off without them. If the money required to billet them could be converted to improving the services it would be a better investment of public funds.

I witnessed a scene in the sheds today that deserves mention in my journal. I was attending to a man who came over on the last ship from Sligo. His name is Pat Coady. While I was bending over him he gave a start as his eye caught the sight of a man they were lifting into the adjoining berth. Wasted and sallow as he was I recognized him. He was the leader of a small group of Orangemen who lived just outside of Palmerston's estate. His name was Eldon Stanhope and for a long time he and Coady had been at odds. One day at the market place they got into a wild brawl. Coady was a powerful man and laid Stanhope out on the turf. Coady's eldest son, who could have taken on the two of them together, taunted Stanhope after the fight. A few days later Stanhope led a party that beat Coady's eldest son and his four other boys nigh to death. This made the feud all the more bitter and an exchange of insults and challenges continued. Here were the two mortal enemies side by side, both of them laid low by the fever. Stanhope looked very weary so I held up his head and gave him some cordial after which he fell asleep. Meanwhile Father O'Hare, who knew the two of them, came along and we waited to see what would happen.

After a few minutes Stanhope opened his eyes and gazed around till they fell on Coady who had been watching him for some time. The glitter of the old fire sprang into Stanhope's eyes and a slight flush passed over his white face. But the stern, hard look gradually faded. He suddenly held out a bony hand and spoke in a rasping throaty voice: "Is that yerself, Pat Coady? Will you shake hands with me?"

"It's meself" said Coady, "and it's glad and proud I am to do the same. We'll let bygones be bygones."

They both recovered from the fever and planned to go together to homestead in Upper Canada. Coady's five sons got jobs on the boats between Quebec and Montreal. Their mother died on the ocean. Stanhope was alone.

It is estimated that there are over two thousand now in the fever sheds and in the other temporary shelters on the island.

June 20. Several of the clergy and one of the doctors have come down with the fever. I feel that my turn will come for I have been very close to the sources of contagion for a long time. I spoke to Doctor Fenwick, Doctor Douglas' chief assistant, about continuing the work here if I do not succumb to the fever. He told me that there was plenty of work for extra hands at all times. He mentioned, for example, the little herd of cattle that needed tending and a lighthouse that had no regular keeper, as well as all kinds of repair work. I am willing to take on any kind of work that comes within the range of my talents if I can only remain here.

June 23. My time has come. I woke from a fitful sleep this morning with every bone in my body aching. Someone must have told Doctor Douglas for he came and gave me some medicine with orders to remain in bed. The medicine eased my suffering enough to allow me to pick up my journal once again. I have a compelling urge to continue telling my story as long as I am able to write. If they move me to the fever sheds it will likely be the end of it all. This could happen tonight or tomorrow morning.

June 24. They did not move me. I stayed in my cot all day. Since I am exposing the clergy to the risk of catching whatever I have, it would not be right to remain here. Perhaps they will allow me to move into the little lean-to where Eileen died in my arms.

Father McGoran suggested that I receive the last rites. Having gratefully accepted the suggestion I prepared myself to take part in the ritual. Those who make the rounds of the fever sheds see it performed dozens of times every day, never without bringing peace and composure and even physical healing, at times, to the recipient. In my case it blotted out much of the mental anguish of the past two weeks and replaced it with a feeling of tranquillity in spite of the racking pains of the fever.

There is much more to be written but every effort is painful and my writing is, I know, getting illegible. Perhaps it will be possible to take it up again during one of the respites that fever patients experience even when they are near the end.

June 25. After a very bad night my condition improved somewhat around noon hour today. After taking a cup of tea and a bit of broth it looked as if the fever might subside. But it picked up again this evening. My body is beginning to show swellings. The most distressful of all the symptoms is a very disagreeable odour which develops in the late stage of the fever. It is now beginning to show, in my case. This signals the end. Doctor Fenwick was here today but it was plain from his outward expression that it is too late now for medicines.

Reverend Mountain came to see me. May God reward him for his kindness! He said a prayer over me and said he'd be back. This evening I asked Father O'Hare to look after this little book and my few belongings for I don't think I'll be able to write any more. I am leaving in it the address of my uncle, Dan O'Connor who lives near Montreal. I also left a note with my cousins, Ellen and Bridget, telling them how to get to Uncle Dan's for I fear that they will be alone in the world. Uncle Jeremiah will never recover from the damage the fever has done to his mind.

This writing looks very shaky. In reverent memory of all who have perished in this holocaust and of all who have suffered in any way, as well as to all those who have spent themselves in a heroic effort to help us, I dedicate the message in this little book.

Farewell,

Gerald Keegan

7

Closing of the Journal

June 27. I, Father Tom O'Hare, am adding the following notes to my dear young friend's journal at his request. He is still alive, in and out of periods of delirium and I don't think that he will last long. I spent almost all of last night reading the journal through. I feel, like Gerald, that it is urgent for the world to know about what is going on. It is probably the only weapon we have – the only way to fight the evil forces that are destroying so many of our people. The little book is a treasure of factual information. Its only defect, as Gerald himself wrote, is that it falls short of the full reality, of the depth of misery to which hundreds of thousands have been reduced.

June 28. Some victims of the fever get struck down quickly. Others linger on. Gerald has been sick for almost a week now. At this stage he has all the symptoms of impending dissolution. He is supposed to be in the fever sheds, but in deference to a last request of his, I got him transported to a little tree in the thicket beside Eileen's grave. It is a beautiful day and the weather, even at night, is mild and warm.

In one of his periods of complete consciousness he asked for the journal, intending to add another note. But it fell from his hands. He smiled a smile of resignation as I picked it up from the ground. His gaze is frequently fixed on the little cross over the grave. I am stealing some time from my duties to be with him at the end.

This evening there was a glorious sunset. To the north the rolling hills of the Laurentian mountains stand out silhouetted by the setting sun. The whole scene punctuated by rugged Cape Tourmente. Nature's show is in marked contrast with the scenes of death and destruction on the island – the work of man. Darkness gradually crept over the scene, the cross faded from view and I left my young friend wrapped in a blanket by the tree. Several of us will visit him during the night.

June 29. Early in the morning I found that Keegan's face and limbs were badly swollen. It would be a matter of hours, I felt, before his ordeal would be over. He was conscious only for very short periods of time. Shortly after noon his uncle, Dan O'Connor arrived. How he got here I cannot imagine for it is strictly forbidden for anyone, except those engaged in some kind of service, to come to the island. I found O'Connor looking very disconsolate, leaning over his nephew trying to talk to him. Father McGoran was with him. Keegan finally regained consciousness and recognized his uncle. As near as I can recall these are the words they exchanged.

"May God bless you, uncle. What made you come to this awful place?" he moaned.

"I came to do anything I can, even to carry you away from here. I'll take you with me to my farm."

"Thank you, uncle, it's too late." Keegan smiled sorrowfully.

Those were his last words. Late in the afternoon he breathed his last. Though I am close to the dying at all

I lifted him in my arms and carried him out of the shed. I was powerful strong when I was young, and tho' he was tall and broad-shouthered he was wasted to skin and bone. I laid him down in the shade of a tree, for the sun was hot. He didn't look at the river or the hills beyant, but fixed his eyes on a spot that I took to be a burying-place. "Go back," he whispered, "and bring the bag below my berth." I went, and found a woman had already been put in the poor bed I had lifted him out of. I reached for the bag and took it to him. Pointing to a spot in the burying-place he told me to go there and I would see a grave with a cross at its head and the name Aileen cut on it. "You can read?" "Yes" says I. I did his bidding and coming back told him I had found the grave. "Promise me, you'll bury me beside that grave." I promised him. "Open the bag and you'll find in it a little book." I reached it to him. "Take it," says he, "there are pages in it I would tear out were I able. Let it go. Save the book; it will tell to those now unborn what Irish men and women have suffered in this summer of sorrow."

From the original journal

times, I stood over this young man with tears in my eyes. He gave his life for his suffering people. He is a symbol of the hope that we must all cling to in these dark times. I got Doctor Fenwick to certify his death and with his uncle's help prepared the body for burial. The sun was setting as usual with a glorious display of colours. We laid his body to rest next to Eileen's. Tomorrow I will add his name to the cross that marks the grave. His precious little journal I will turn over to O'Connor. To those who may have the privilege of reading it I wish to say that it was truly an inspiration and an honour to have known this young man.

Signed: Father Tom O'Hare

To understand the mortality figures on Grosse Ile it must be understood that hundreds died while waiting on board ship for the medical examination. A great many died while being transported to shore and on the beach where they were laid. A large number, demented by fever or horror-stricken over the conditions of the fever sheds, escaped to the wooded areas of the island where they died. Corpses were found all over the island. They were buried where they were found. At the height of the fever there were over a hundred deaths a day. The count of bodies that was finally begun did not start till well on in June when almost half of the victims were already buried. All these facts indicate that the official count on the monument, 5,424, is grossly underestimated. It is believed by some, including clergy who ministered to the dying, that 15,000 would be a more accurate count. It must be remembered also that the government tried to censor reports about the magnitude of the disaster at Grosse Ile. Keeping the recorded number of casualties as low as possible fitted in with the policy of officialdom.

A. Bechard

8

The Recovery of the Journal

Had it not been for Dan O'Connor's determination to get to Grosse Ile to see his nephew, Keegan's journal would likely have been lost or destroyed. The story of his return trip to the quarantine station was put together, after many interviews, by the original publishers of the diary. Up until quite recently there were some descendants of the original settlers in the Huntingdon area of the Chateauguay Basin who could still remember hearing details about the journal and about O'Connor's adventuresome trip. As might be expected there were different versions of the latter. But there was a consistency about them that left no doubt about the truth of the principal details. The following paragraphs relate the story as pieced together by James Mangan.

O'Connor and his wife, Honora, were cutting hay with little iron hooks in a field about a stone's throw from their farmhouse not far from Huntingdon. In the quiet, dead heat of the afternoon O'Connor suddenly straightened up and told Honora that he had a strange feeling about a third person being present in the field. Honora felt that it was the heat that was getting to him so they stopped work and sat in the shade of a small tree.

No sooner had they sat down than they spied two skeletonlike creatures standing near a large stump about fifty yards away. They were two young girls though they had the faces of older women. The bones of their faces stretched their tight drawn skin. Eyes sunk in hollow sockets made them look like ghosts. Nobody made a move or spoke for several minutes.

Finally the two strange creatures approached and spoke in a plaintive voice, addressing O'Connor as Uncle Dan. Thinking that they were two demented children he asked them why they called him Uncle. They gave their names as Ellen and Bridget and said that their father's name was Jeremiah O'Connor. On being asked where Jeremiah was they related what happened including the fact that their cousin, Gerald, was down with the fever.

It sounded so incredible that O'Connor and his wife couldn't quite believe it. Perhaps it was all make-believe, they thought. But still it sounded truthful, though Jeremiah had written them a letter about three months previously without any mention of coming to Canada. All doubts were removed when one of the girls handed O'Connor a letter written by his nephew, Gerald, asking him to take care of them. The letter explained that their father was no longer able to do so.

The two girls were taken to the farmhouse and given tender and affectionate care by Honora. Dan determined to leave on the next stage coach for Montreal on his way to Grosse Ile. Bridget begged him not to go for, with all the sickness there, it would be the death of him. But nothing could change his mind.

After a light meal of nourishing food and a few hours in a comfortable bed the girls were able to explain how they made the long trip from the quarantine station. As soon as the fever left them they were put on a boat for Montreal with Keegan's precious note and directions on how to get to the O'Connor farm when they got off the boat. They were two days on the boat without any food except what they could beg from others who had very little to give. Many other children, a lot of them orphans, were on the same boat. Like the ocean vessels, the river boats provided no comforts or conveniences of any kind. Finding a place on deck to spend the night was a problem for everybody.

Faint and sick and starving, like many of the other passengers, they arrived at the emigrant landing dock in Montreal. Completely bewildered and very downhearted they wished that death would deliver them from their misery. They had the letter telling them where to go but who would help? A policeman ordered them off the dock just as a Protestant clergyman came along and intervened. They showed him the note written by Keegan. After reading it the clergyman took them to a boat tied up in the canal. He went to the Captain and asked him to take the two girls to Beauharnois. He offered to pay their passage. The Captain took them on board, refusing to accept any money. The kindly minister gave them some money and slipped away before they could thank him.

Landed at Beauharnois the girls were completely lost. Everybody was speaking French. They approached a man who was loading flour onto a wagon. He read the note and fortunately for them he was English speaking. His name was McGregor. He said he'd like to help them but was afraid of the risk of catching the fever. Telling them to sit on the back of the wagon, he entered a tavern. When he came out he drove off with the two girls and let them sleep on the hay in his barn that night. Next morning he called them at sun-up, gave them a bowl of porridge and milk and gave them directions to O'Connor's farm. Though he told them that it was about an hour's walk from his place they took all forenoon to get there.

Coming back to O'Connor himself, the stagecoach dropped him at an inn not far from where the ship landed the emigrants. All the talk at the inn was about the fever – the plague as they called it. It must have been very much like the situation on Grosse Ile for hundreds were dying every week. There was no boat for Quebec till the following day, so O'Connor decided to have a look around. The sight of all the confusion and movement in and around long rows of sheds down towards the river led him to try to get nearer. But he was stopped by a policeman who turned him back. He knew about the sheds for the whole countryside for miles around spoke of little else. But it was shocking to be face to face with long rows of shelters built to receive the ever-increasing flood of fever victims. Clergymen, doctors and nurses and a group of nuns in grey habits could be seen attending to the needs of the sick and dying. He came across a little boy lying on the ground. A girl, deathly pale, with sunken eyes, was leaning over him. On asking if he could do anything for her, the girl thanked him. The boy, who was her brother, was dying. O'Connor went and told a policeman who concluded that they must have escaped from the sheds. With an oath he marched towards them and uttered some harsh words of reprimand just as the boy's body quivered and relaxed in death. The girl refused to be comforted. The policeman got two men with a cart to take the body away. They tried to get the girl to move but found that she too had died suddenly. The men with the burial cart said that scenes like this were common.

Next morning O'Connor boarded a steamer for Quebec. Just beyond Three Rivers another boat hove into sight going up-river. The lower deck was packed with emigrants, all in rags, peering out of sunken eyes. Their sharp features and deathly pallor made them look like ghosts. The wind carried the odours from the emigrant

ship and, though it was about three hundred yards
distant, the air was stifling. A member of the crew told
O'Connor that none of these ships reached Montreal
without a row of dead bodies on one corner of the deck
and that many emigrants would end up in the fever sheds
at Montreal.

When O'Connor landed in Quebec he took a room in
a small inn near the docks. Next morning he asked the
innkeeper how he could get to Grosse Ile. On being told
that people don't go to Grosse Ile, they only leave it or
else get buried there, he persisted and explained why.
The innkeeper told him how to get to the dock where
the quarantine boat was tied up, warning him that he
didn't have a chance of getting passage. A sentry
challenged him as he neared the dock. While he was
pleading with the sentry a tall soldierly looking cleric
approached and asked what was going on. He explained
that the sentry was doing him a favour in holding him
back for Grosse Ile meant danger if not certain death for
anyone who went there. The cleric, who turned out to
be none other than Reverend George Mountain,
relented when he learned that the reason for the visit was
to see Gerald Keegan. After reminding O'Connor that
his nephew might be already dead, he led him past the
sentry, telling the latter that he was bringing along a new
assistant with him. Their boat rode out with considerable
speed on the tide and an hour later the fleet of ships in
the harbour and the long rows of fever sheds came into
view. He led O'Connor to where his nephew lay, alive
but unconscious. The brief exchange between the two
has already been described in the notes that Father
O'Hare added to the journal.

After helping to bury his nephew, O'Connor
immediately set out to get information about his brother,
Jeremiah. What he found out was most distressing. A
severe bout of the fever, together with all the other trials

he endured, left him crippled in mind and in body. He was like a man walking in his sleep, capable of doing a few very simple chores but out of touch with reality. At the request of Keegan, Doctor Douglas was kind enough to give him a small cabin beside a garden which he was helping to tend. With him was the keeper of the lighthouse who kept an eye on him.

On being told where to find him O'Connor went to the cabin and found him lying on his cot, staring at the ceiling. Despite all efforts to attract his attention he failed to recognize his brother. It was a heartrending experience to watch him lying there so unresponsive. Hoping against hope, hour after hour, merely underlined the futility of trying to rouse him. At sundown he got up and, with a wild look in his eyes, ambled down to the lighthouse.

Standing at the edge of the water, his long white hair blowing in the wind, he gazed out at the river. Raising his right hand he waved at whatever he saw and stood staring fixedly for a long time.

The lighthouse keeper explained that this happened every night just after sunset. In his vision he saw emigrant ships going by and he even counted the number of ghostly passengers crowded on the deck of each vessel. The keeper said that Doctor Douglas did not want to have him sent on to Quebec or Montreal until arrangements could be made to have him cared for.

Leaving his brother to his nightly tryst with the ghosts of his past, Dan O'Connor tearfully left the lighthouse determined to come back in the near future and bring Jeremiah with him. Doctor Douglas had assured him that he would be well looked after in the meantime and that it would not be advisable to have him travel upriver on an emigrant ship in his present condition.

Approaching the sheds he was challenged by a guard who suspected that he might be an escaping fever victim. Inquiries about how to leave the island led to the con-

clusion that the only way was to get passage on one of
the ships. Having seen a few of these on the way from
Montreal, he was determined to find some other way.
Contact with any of the officials might lead to further
trouble.

The nearest point to the mainland was over towards
the northwest corner of the island. Not far from the
burial trenches two gravediggers appeared with shovels
over their shoulders, carrying lanterns. They were French
speaking and it was only with a combination of signs and
words that O'Connor could explain his problem. They
told him that there were guards all over the place and
that the only way of getting off the island was by
travelling on the emigrant ships. One of them, however,
suggested that there might be a way. His fellow worker
was about to slip across to his home on the mainland
under cover of darkness. By choosing the right place the
guards could be avoided. After a worthwhile reward was
offered it was agreed that an attempt would be made.

While waiting for a signal from the man who agreed
to take him to the mainland, O'Connor took stock of the
burial system. During the short time, less than an hour,
that he was waiting, two cart loads of bodies arrived. This
seemed to confirm what he had been told about the
death rate on the island being from 50 to 100 a day when
things were at their worst. He noted that the trenches
were about a hundred feet long and a few feet deep and
they were dug in parallel rows. Unfortunately they were
not deep enough to protect the bodies from the hordes
of rodents that infested the island.

When the Frenchman signalled he went and followed
him to a clump of bushes at the water's edge where a
boat was concealed. They slid out on the tide and a small
sail was hoisted. With the added help of a pair of home-
made oars they reached the other shore where the boat
was immediately hidden in the bushes. With a parting

"Bon voyage" the owner of the boat set out along a well worn path towards his destination.

In spite of the breeze it was a warm night. After a thorough scrubbing in the sand together with a soaking in the river, O'Connor lay down for a rest until daybreak. Early in the morning he walked to the nearest farmhouse to see if he could get some food. With a threatening gesture the farmer ordered him away, suspecting him of being an escaped fever victim. Not daring to risk another like adventure he set out on the long walk to Quebec. Just before noon he came across a man who was hauling small logs with a horse. He signalled his need for food whereupon the man opened a sack tied to the horse's harness and handed him a meat sandwich. Expressing his deep gratitude to the good Samaritan he sat by the river to enjoy what turned out to be the most appetizing food he had tasted in a long time.

Late that night, footsore and weary, he arrived at the inn where he had already lodged. The inkeeper immediately led him to a back room.

"Stay right here," he said, "and for God's sake don't show yourself. If any of my customers knew that you came from the island they'd clear out right away. I'll bring you some food."

After supper the innkeeper returned to hear the story of the visit to Grosse Ile. He sympathized with his guest on hearing the bad news and reminded him that terrible things were happening to the poor emigrants in Quebec, in Montreal and all the way up the waterway which was marked by a trail of graveyards.

That night turned out to be a memorable one. By the light of a little oil lamp, O'Connor painstakingly read his nephew's journal. Though every muscle in his body ached from the long walk, he devoured the contents of the little book and put it aside only in the early hours of the morning when the lamp ran out of oil. Even after hearing all kinds of news about the troubles his people were going through, he was deeply moved and singularly impressed by the message in the little book. In fact he realized that he knew very little about the whole situation until he read the journal. Though his visit to Grosse Ile brought him face to face with scenes of misery and desolation that shook him to the very core of his being he reaped one precious benefit from his adventure. The journal was a living message, a treasured possession, from the young man he had come to save and, indeed, from all the poor, unfortunate emigrants. If it had not been for this, his visit to the island would have been a complete and very bitter failure.

The rest of his story is very brief. He got passage on one of the ships to Montreal. For two days and one night he shared the horrors of being confined to a floating pesthouse with several hundred Irish who had come to Canada from Liverpool. About fifteen passengers died before reaching Montreal.

He had suffered many trials and deprivations and had faced many dangers during his lifetime but nothing could remotely compare with the intensity of the human misery and degradation that he witnessed at the quarantine station and at other places along the way.

He was fortunate in not catching the fever but took the precaution of sleeping on a bundle of hay in a small shed adjoining his house for a few days in case he might be carrying the contagion. Later on in the summer, when the fever epidemic had subsided and ships were no longer arriving, he returned to Grosse Ile to visit his brother. Since he was doing as well as could be expected at the little jobs assigned to him, Doctor Douglas suggested that he be left there and that he would keep him under his personal care.

About six weeks later Doctor Douglas forwarded a message announcing that Jeremiah O'Connor was gravely ill. By the time Dan arrived at Grosse Ile, he was already dead. The body was brought to the little cemetery on Finn's farm where a few of the first settlers in that area were buried.

Besides Keegan's journal O'Connor brought back a few other souvenirs of his sad pilgrimage to the quarantine station. Eileen's shawl, a lock of Jeremiah's prematurely white hair, a few books belonging to Gerald and a beautiful Celtic cross, carved out of Connemara marble, a wedding present from the people of his native village, were poignant reminders of tragic events in the lives of members of his own family. In a special little trench, a stone's throw from the house, these souvenirs were placed, inside a wooden box, as a safeguard in case of fire or of other risks of their being destroyed or removed from the premises. When little groups gathered, as they did regularly to hear the reading of the journal, the other souvenirs were always laid out on the kitchen table, silent reminders of a summer of sorrow.

9

Epilogue

Greater love than this no man hath. . . .

On the pedestal of a monument in City Hall Square, Quebec, there is an impressive bronze plaque erected to the memory of Elzear Alexandre Tachereau, later known as Cardinal Tachereau. The plaque shows a scene at Grosse Ile. A priest and some nuns are attending the sick and dying. (Representing nuns at Grosse Ile seems to be an error. They are not mentioned in any of the records.) In the background, out in the harbour, one of the emigrant sailing vessels is shown. Tachereau was a young priest, newly ordained, when he volunteered for service at the Grosse Ile quarantine station during the disastrous summer months of 1847. The plaque was intended as a tribute, not only to young Father Tachereau, but to all the clergy who offered their services during that fateful period.

When Tachereau and his companion, Edward John Horan, left for Grosse Ile they were fully aware of the risk they were taking. There would be little hope of escaping the contagion. Though hunger and poor sanitation contributed more than anything else to the progress of the disease it spared no class, neither rich nor poor, neither the well-fed nor the hungry. It often struck with lightning swiftness. In Ireland, for example, whole families were known to have perished overnight. Their shielings had to be levelled over their bodies to bury them. On Grosse Ile thousands of the emigrants were easy victims of its ravages, weakened and starved as they were after the ocean voyage. Into this world of contagion came clergymen, both Catholic and Anglican, who joined with the doctors and other attendants in ministering to the needs of the mass of suffering humanity they found there.

Many among the clergy who did not serve on the island tried to find homes for orphans. One of the Irish emigrants recalled, many years after that fateful summer, a touching incident that took place in the Basilica in Quebec. It was during Sunday Mass. At the time for the sermon the priest, Monsignor Baillargeon, led two children with him into the pulpit. The parishioners were told that there were hundreds of children like these two, left homeless, after losing parents and relatives on the ocean and at the quarantine station. Monsignor Baillargeon appealed to them to take the children into their homes.

The response of the people was a joy to his heart. The following Sunday and for many Sundays after, people from Quebec and the farms and settlements down the river asked to take one or more orphans into their homes. The rectory became a clearing-house for orphans. When they overcame their initial shyness they became playful and somewhat noisy but this didn't seem to disturb their generous host. In fact it was with regret that he saw the last one leave. A few were taken into English-speaking families but the vast majority found homes among the predominantly French-speaking population. Many of them kept their own names. This explains how, all over the province of Quebec, we find people named Kelly or Murphy or O'Brien who cannot speak a word of English. In a generation or so the Irish orphans literally became French Canadian, not merely in language but in their whole cultural identity. This was due mainly to the fact that they were fully accepted as members of the families that adopted them.

Other priests in the country parishes were inspired by Monsignor Baillargeon's example and came to him offering to take orphans for adoption among their parishioners. One priest, who called at the rectory on a Sunday afternoon remarked that "there seemed to be children running all over the house". Having heard about the Monsignor's method of advertising, the pastor of the little church at Valcartier brought three orphans with him to the pulpit. Pointing to the singular beauty of expression of the children he said: "You must wonder why I am showing you these little ones. Well, they are orphans. Their parents are buried at Grosse Ile. We cannot find any of their relatives. They are now alone and abandoned. I appeal to you with the words of Christ himself: 'I was a stranger and you took me in.' I am asking you to take these children into your homes. I need hardly remind you that you can expect no earthly reward for an act of charity of this kind. Your reward will be far beyond what can be measured in terms of earthly compensation."

After Mass there was a choice of at least a dozen homes for the three children.

Those who got quarantine clearance at Grosse Ile went on to Quebec, Montreal, Ottawa, Kingston, Toronto and even to the American border at Detroit as was the case with William Ford, father of Henry, whose wife, Mary, was buried at the quarantine station. For those who were not quarantined the only medical examination they had consisted in sticking out their tongue as they passed rapidly in front of the medical officer who had to go through five or six hundred at a time on some of the ships. The result was that many who should have been hospitalized were loaded onto the boats going up-river to Quebec and Montreal. In their weakened condition they were easy victims of both cholera and typhus. The ships landed their ghostly cargoes at the east end of Montreal, the area known as Point St Charles. Here another mass tragedy, matching that of Grosse Ile in the extent and intensity of suffering from the deadly fever, took place in Canada's largest city.

At Montreal, the government finally erected three sheds 150 feet long by about 40 feet wide. As thousands of the sick emigrants continued to land, eleven more sheds had to be erected. The mortality along the river bank at Point St Charles was appalling.

An article in *The Gazette*, Montreal, September 5, 1847, gives a description of the scene at Point St Charles fever sheds when the courageous volunteers arrived there:

> In the hastily erected emergency sheds the people were dying by the score in the crowded sheds, in the stench and heat, desperately neglected. When there were enough attendants they were hastily tossed into shallow pits nearby when they succumbed to the fever. In all the history of Montreal there is no story so poignant. There were hundreds of orphaned children. Many of the little ones had to be pulled from the arms of a parent who had suddenly died. Older ones were wandering around frantically looking for parents who were already buried in the pits. The scene in the children's shed was beyond description.

One of the most pathetic features of the total catastrophe, both in Ireland and on the ocean as well as in Canada, was the large number of children left friendless and alone in the wake of the famine and fever. Those who were old enough to realize what was happening were often found in a pitiful state of prostration beside the body of a parent, brother, sister or other near relative. Those who were too young to grasp the meaning of death were frequently left, sometimes for hours, crying frantically beside the body of a mother who would never again respond to their need for attention. For the dying parent it was a severe shock to realize that a child would be left abandoned in the frightful atmosphere of a fever shed. According to notes written by some of the clergy there were over six hundred orphaned at Grosse Ile alone. Including casualties on the ships and at all the places in Canada where the fever struck, there must have been over two thousand.

All the major settlements in Lower and in Upper Canada were touched by the plague. Kingston and Ottawa, for example, had to set up emergency facilities to care for the hundreds of sick and dying who got that far inland. In the midst of the panic-ridden populations there was no lack of self-sacrificing individuals to render emergency services to the stricken emigrants.

A report in the *Montreal Immigrant Society Bulletin* in 1848 had the following comment:

From Grosse Ile, the great charnel house of victimized humanity, up to Port Sarnia and all along the St Lawrence and the Great Lakes, wherever the tide of immigration extended, are to be found the final resting places of the sons and daughters of Erin — one unbroken chain of graves where rest fathers and mothers, sisters and brothers, without a stone to mark the spot. I do not know that the history of our times has a parallel for this Irish exodus. . . It was the forced expulsion and panic rush of a stricken people and it was attended by frightful scenes of suffering and death.

Toronto was considered a step on the way to the American border which the majority of the Irish hoped to reach. There also, many succumbed to fever and typhoid. Many of the citizens were so afraid of disease that they left for the country. Since the majority of the citizens of Toronto were from England, or at least of English descent, the influx of Irish was met with rather violent resentment. Even if they had not brought the fever they were not welcome. They were warned by placards that they were not wanted when there was a question of employment or housing. Paradoxically, however, the Irish clergy and prominent, well-known lay people were highly thought of in general.

It would not be proper to end this story without at least a brief reference to the survivors of famine, pestilence and the hardships of travel. In their search for ways and means of earning a living they got no help of any kind from the government. In fact they were completely rejected by the predominantly British population of Upper Canada. Being Irish and being poor they were not wanted. It was almost impossible to get a bit of land fit for cultivation. All the choice lands had already been given to the united Empire Loyalists or selectively distributed by land agents to people they considered loyal to the Crown. The only alternative was to clear patches of land in the dense forests or else take on slave labour on the railroads, in the mines or in the forests. But they were used to hardship and they succeeded in earning a living while making substantial contributions to the development of Canada. A remarkable number of them and of their descendants rose to positions of distinction in Church and State and in commerce and industry. All who could possibly do so crossed the border into the United States and it was there that they distinguished themselves as leaders much more than in Canada where promotion depended almost entirely upon membership in certain societies that were identified with those who wielded power, both politically and socially.